Foundations of Streaming Broadcast Media

Foundations of Streaming Broadcast Media

Understanding The Basics

Myron A. Raney, Ph.D.

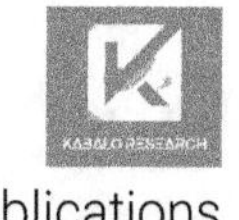

Kabalo Research Publications

This book is dedicated to all the future generations of creative minds:
"He's gifted them with the know-how needed for carving, designing, weaving, and embroidering in blue, purple, and scarlet fabrics, and in fine linen. They can make anything and design anything" (Exodus 35:35, MSG).

CONTENTS

CONTENTS

Have you ever wondered how you can enjoy your favorite movies, TV shows, music, and sports events anytime, anywhere, with just a few taps on your screen? Have you ever marveled at the sheer convenience and accessibility of streaming services that have revolutionized the way we consume media? If so, then prepare yourself for a journey into the captivating world of audio and video streaming.

In this book, we will embark on a thrilling adventure exploring the technical, operational, legal, and monetization aspects of the media streaming landscape. Together, we will dive deep into the vast ocean of information, uncovering hidden gems and untold stories that shape the very fabric of this fascinating world.

But before we set sail, allow me to introduce myself. I am Myron Raney, a social science researcher, social entrepreneur, documentary filmmaker, nonprofit executive, and the Chairman and CEO of a broadcast media streaming network. With my extensive experience and expertise in the field, I am thrilled to share with you the knowledge and insights that I have gained over the years.

Now, let us embark on this remarkable journey together. Imagine standing at the crossroads of technology and creativity, witnessing first-hand the artistry and innovation behind every stream. Picture yourself peering behind the curtain, where the magic of digitization and compression transforms raw audio and video files into seamless streams that captivate our senses.

In the pages that follow, we will delve into the fundamental principles of audio and video streaming. We will unravel the intricate web of acronyms and technicalities that govern this ever-expanding universe. From codecs and bit rates to adaptive streaming and buffering, no stone will be left unturned as we decipher the language of the streaming world.

But this book is not just a technical manual. It is a holistic exploration of the streaming media industry. We will explore the business side of streaming, uncovering the secrets to building and running a successful streaming platform. We will discuss the myriad of legal considerations that shape the industry, ensuring that you are equipped with the knowledge to navigate this complex landscape with confidence.

Moreover, we will journey into the realm of monetization, where creativity and commerce collide. Together, we will uncover the various revenue streams available to content creators and streaming platform owners, empowering you to turn your passion for streaming into a lucrative venture.

Throughout the chapters, I will weave in stories and anecdotes from my personal experiences in the field. These real-life examples will paint a vivid picture of the challenges, triumphs, and lessons learned along the way. I want you to feel as if you are by my side, experiencing the exhilaration and occasional setbacks that come with navigating this ever-evolving industry.

Whether you are a student delving into the world of streaming for the first time or a seasoned professional seeking to expand your horizons, this book has something for everyone. It is a comprehensive guide, carefully designed to cater to your needs and provide you with the tools to thrive in the enthralling realm of audio and video streaming.

So, dear reader, I invite you to fasten your seatbelt and get ready for an unforgettable journey. Together, we will conquer the peaks and valleys of the streaming mountain, unlocking the secrets that lie within. By the end of this book, you will be equipped with a wealth of knowledge and a newfound appreciation for the wonders of streaming media.

Let the adventure begin!

1

Chapter 1: Exploring the Evolution and Influence of Streaming Media

What Is Streaming Media?

To commence, let us establish the precise meaning of streaming media. Fundamentally, streaming media entails the transmission of multimedia content, such as audio or video, in a continuous and uninterrupted manner via a network. In contrast to conventional media formats, where content is downloaded and stored locally on a device prior to playback, streaming media enables real-time consumption sans the necessity of downloading. This feat is made possible via the utilization of protocols, such as HTTP (Hypertext Transfer Protocol) or RTSP (Real-Time Streaming Protocol), which enable the transmission of data in small packets as they are received and rendered by the playback device.

One of the primary benefits of streaming media lies in its capacity to offer instantaneous access to content. Gone are the days of waiting for a video or audio file to download before enjoying it. With streaming, users can commence watching a movie or listening to music within seconds, leading to significant time and storage savings. Furthermore, users can effortlessly explore a vast array of content and sample different genres and formats without committing to a full download. It is this convenience and accessibility that has contributed to the widespread popularity of streaming media.

Additionally, streaming media provides an unprecedented level of flexibility and customization. Traditional media formats typically provide static and fixed content, allowing little room for personalization. However, streaming media platforms often afford personalized recommendations and curated playlists, thereby tailoring the user experience to individual preferences. This enhances user engagement and satisfaction as viewers and listeners are presented with content aligned with their tastes and interests. Moreover, streaming media platforms may offer interactive features, permitting users to comment, engage in discussions, or even participate in live events, fostering a sense of community and connectedness.

Another notable advantage of streaming media lies in the sheer breadth of content available. Traditional media's distribution channels and physical limitations have frequently restricted the variety and accessibility of content. However, streaming media platforms can aggregate content from numerous sources, offering users a vast library of movies, TV shows, music, podcasts, and more. This democratization of content has empowered creators and artists to reach a global audience, bypassing traditional gatekeepers and distribution channels. It has also given rise to niche genres and independent creators who may have previously encountered difficulty in finding an audience.

Nonetheless, streaming media is not without its limitations and drawbacks. One of the most significant concerns pertains to content ownership and control. Unlike physical media or downloaded files, streaming media content relies on the availability of the platform or service provider. Should a platform decide to remove a specific movie or album from its library, users are left with no means of accessing that content. Similarly, if a streaming service ceases operation, the content it hosted may become permanently inaccessible. This transitory nature and reliance on external services can unsettle users who value ownership and control over their media.

Another potential disadvantage of streaming media is tied to the quality of the content. While streaming platforms strive to deliver high-quality audio and video, the experience can be compromised by factors such as internet speed or network congestion. Insufficient bandwidth can lead to buffering, which disrupts the smooth playback of content and diminishes the overall viewing or listening experience. Moreover, streaming media frequently makes use of data compression techniques to reduce file sizes, which can result in a decline in picture or sound quality compared to the original source material. For discerning viewers or audiophiles, this compromise in quality may be a significant drawback.

Furthermore, access to streaming media often hinges upon the availability of a reliable internet connection. In areas where internet access is limited or unreliable, streaming media may not be a feasible option. This creates a digital divide that perpetuates disparities in access to information and entertainment. Additionally, the reliance on internet connectivity implies that users are susceptible to potential service disruptions, be it due to network outages, bandwidth limitations, or other technical issues. This unpredictability can prove frustrating for users accustomed to a seamless and uninterrupted streaming experience.

In conclusion, streaming media has ushered in a new era of audio and video consumption. Its ability to deliver content in real-time, coupled with the convenience, flexibility, and variety it affords, has revolutionized the way we engage with media. While there are advantages to streaming media, such as instant access to content, personalization, and a vast library of options, it is crucial to consider certain disadvantages, including the lack of ownership and control over content, potential compromises in quality, and the reliance on internet connectivity. As the landscape of streaming media continues to evolve, it is imperative for users and content creators alike to navigate these opportunities and challenges with an informed perspective. By comprehending the intricacies of streaming media, we can fully appreciate its transformative potential in the realm of audio and video consumption.

Evolution of Streaming Media

The development and progress of streaming media have been re-markable since its inception. In its early stages, streaming was primarily used to transmit radio and television broadcasts through the airwaves. Television networks would transmit their programming via analog signals, which viewers could receive using antennas.

The introduction of cable television revolutionized the way media was consumed. By transmitting signals through coaxial cables, cable providers expanded the range of available channels, offering viewers a wider selection of entertainment options. This marked a significant step toward the democratization of media, as it enabled diverse content to be delivered directly to people's homes.

However, the true breakthrough occurred with the emergence of the internet. The public's introduction to the World Wide Web in the early 1990s opened up a whole new realm of possibilities for media consumption. The internet facilitated the transmission of data packets, enabling the real-time delivery of audio and video content without requiring downloads or buffering.

Initially, streaming media was constrained by low-quality audio and video formats due to internet bandwidth limitations. Technological advancements and the subsequent increase in internet speeds propelled streaming media to evolve rapidly. The advent of broadband internet in the late 1990s was a transformative milestone. Faster speeds allowed users to stream higher quality audio and video content, bringing the concept of "on-demand" media into reality.

The early 2000s witnessed the emergence of prominent players in the streaming industry. Companies like RealNetworks and Microsoft's Windows Media Player played pivotal roles in developing streaming technologies, enabling users to stream audio and video content directly through web browsers. This accessibility made it easier for content creators to reach wider audiences, eliminating the need for users to download dedicated software to access streaming media.

Around the same time, the rise of peer-to-peer (P2P) file-sharing technology facilitated the distribution of large media files over the internet. Platforms such as Napster and BitTorrent allowed users to share music and movies, albeit often through unauthorized means. Although these platforms faced legal challenges and subsequent shutdowns, they played a critical role in shaping the future of streaming media.

In the mid-2000s, YouTube made a significant entry into the streaming arena. Established in 2005, YouTube swiftly became a global phenomenon, offering users the opportunity to upload, share, and stream video content free of cost. Its user-friendly interface and extensive library of user-generated content made it a go-to platform for online media consumption. The success of YouTube paved the way for the emergence of other streaming platforms, each of which offered unique features and content offerings.

As a result of streaming media's growing popularity, technological advancements enabled even greater innovation. The introduction of high-definition video (HD), and later 4K resolution, provided viewers with a more immersive and visually captivating streaming experience. Similarly, improvements in audio codecs and compression algorithms led to higher-quality audio streaming, supporting formats such as surround sound and other immersive audio options.

In recent years, we have witnessed the ascendance of live streaming, enabling users to broadcast content in real-time to a global audience. This transformation has revolutionized the way we experience events, ranging from concerts and sporting events to news coverage and immersive virtual reality encounters. Live streaming has also fostered a new generation of content creators who can directly engage with viewers and cultivate their own communities.

Looking ahead, it is evident that streaming media will continue to evolve and reshape the media landscape. Technologies such as artificial intelligence and virtual reality stand poised to revolutionize the streaming experience, delivering even more personalized and immersive content. The streaming industry is also embracing new business models, including subscription services and ad-supported platforms, to cater to users' diverse preferences.

In conclusion, the evolution of streaming media has been a captivating journey propelled by technological advancements and dynamic consumer behaviors. From its modest origins as a medium for delivering radio and television signals, streaming media has evolved into a multi-billion dollar industry, offering an array of content options seemingly without limitations. As we venture forth, it will be enthralling to observe how streaming media continues to innovate and reshape the way we consume and interact with media.

Impact of Streaming Media on the Entertainment Industry

Introduction:

The emergence of streaming media has brought about a revolutionary shift in the entertainment industry, fundamentally altering the means by which we access and enjoy content. Gone are the days when dependence on cable subscriptions or physical media was a necessity for viewing our preferred movies and TV shows. The introduction of streaming platforms such as Netflix, Hulu, and Amazon Prime has granted us instant and unrestricted access to an extensive library of content, available anytime and anywhere. This paradigm shift has ushered in notable changes in consumer behavior, content distribution, and revenue models, necessitating a comprehensive understanding of these transformations in order to successfully navigate the evolving landscape of the entertainment industry.

Changes in Consumer Behavior:

Streaming media has completely transformed the manner in which consumers engage with entertainment. Formerly, our consumption options were limited by the constraints of television schedules or the availability of physical media. We found ourselves waiting for the airing of our preferred shows or needing to visit a local video store for DVD rentals. However, the advent of on-demand streaming has granted viewers unparalleled control over what they consume and the time at which they consume it. With the ability to binge-watch entire seasons in a single session or access an extensive compilation of movies and TV shows at their own convenience, consumers now dictate the pace and content of their viewing experiences.

This gradual shift in consumer behavior has concurrently brought about a surge in personalized recommendations and personalized content curation. Streaming platforms leverage user data and sophisticated algorithms to suggest content specifically tailored to individual preferences. This not only enhances the viewer's overall experience but also expose them to previously unknown and diverse content they may not have otherwise discovered. Consequently, streaming media has not singularly attended to preexisting consumer preferences, but also molded their tastes and exposed them to new and novel forms of entertainment.

Changes in Content Distribution:

The ascension of streaming media has disrupted conventional content distribution models. Historically, broadcasters and cable networks determined which shows and movies were made available for our viewing pleasure. However, streaming platforms have democratized content distribution, enabling independent filmmakers and artists to reach a worldwide audience without the reliance on costly production and marketing endeavors.

This democratization of content distribution has likewise prompted the emergence of niche markets and an augmentation of diverse voices within the industry. Streaming platforms serve as a medium through which underrepresented communities and independent filmmakers can showcase their work, frequently posing a challenge to the dominance of mainstream media. Furthermore, the conveniences afforded by online content streaming have dismantled geographical barriers, rendering it possible for international productions to garner a cross-border audience.

Moreover, streaming media has engendered a shift from the traditional linear content release model to a more adaptable and pliable approach. Entire seasons of TV shows are regularly released concurrently, facilitating binge-watching and fan engagement, while original series sporadically release episodes to sustain audience interest. This flexibility in content release has significantly transformed not only our entertainment consumption patterns but has also given birth to novel storytelling formats and narrative structures.

Changes in Revenue Models:

The transformative impact of streaming media has necessitated a comprehensive reassessment of revenue models within the entertainment industry. Traditional models predominantly relied on advertising revenue and box office sales. However, streaming platforms have introduced subscription-based or ad-supported models, providing consumers with inclusive access to an extensive content library in exchange for a monthly fee or exposure to advertising.

This shift has resulted in a decline in DVD and Blu-ray sales, as consumers increasingly gravitate toward the convenience and cost-effectiveness of streaming. Furthermore, streaming platforms have made considerable investments in the production of original content, challenging the established dominion of traditional networks and studios. Consequently, this shift in revenue models has not only fundamentally altered the industry's dynamics, but also opened up new prospects for content creators and artists to secure funding and distribution for their projects.

Conclusion:

The influence of streaming media on the entertainment industry cannot be overstated. Its advent has revolutionized consumer behavior, content distribution, and revenue models, giving rise to a novel era of entertainment consumption. As we progressively embrace the convenience and accessibility afforded by streaming, it is imperative to acknowledge both the opportunities and challenges that accompany this transformative shift. By comprehending the ever-evolving landscape of the entertainment industry, content creators, distributors, and consumers alike can confidently and innovatively navigate the realm of streaming media.

As a dedicated social science researcher, social entrepreneur, documentary filmmaker, nonprofit executive, as well as the Chairman and CEO of a broadcast media streaming network, my commitment remains firmly rooted in exploring the transformative impact of streaming media on various industries. Stay tuned for forthcoming chapters, wherein we delve into the domains of journalism, education, and social activism, thoroughly examining how streaming media has revolutionized these fields.

Types of Streaming Media Platforms

The advent of high-speed internet and the widespread use of smart devices have brought about a significant transformation in the consumption of audio and video content. Streaming media platforms now serve as the primary means for accessing our favorite movies, TV shows, music albums, and live events. As the Chairman and CEO of a broadcast media streaming network, I have personally witnessed the profound impact these platforms have had on the media landscape.

Let us first delve into the realm of on-demand streaming platforms. As the name implies, on-demand streaming offers users the ability to access content at their convenience, either for free or for a fee. Prominent platforms such as Netflix, Hulu, and Amazon Prime Video have emerged as household names, providing an extensive library of movies and TV shows that can be seamlessly streamed. These platforms excel in delivering personalized recommendations based on users' viewing history and preferences, ensuring a consistently engaging experience.

On-demand streaming platforms typically operate on a subscription-based model, wherein users pay a monthly fee in return for unlimited access to the platform's content. This revenue model has proved highly successful in generating a steady stream of income for both content creators and streaming platforms. Moreover, in recent years, we have witnessed the rise of ad-supported on-demand platforms, where users enjoy free access to content while enduring intermittent advertisements.

Convenience stands out as one of the key advantages offered by on-demand streaming platforms. No longer are we bound by the need to hurry home to catch our favorite TV shows at a designated time. With on-demand streaming, we can now enjoy our preferred shows at any time and in any location. Furthermore, these platforms often provide a range of viewing options, enabling us to watch content on smart TVs, laptops, tablets, or smartphones.

Another popular type of streaming media platform is live streaming. Live streaming allows users to view or listen to events as they unfold in real-time. This form of streaming finds particular popularity in sporting events, concerts, conferences, and news broadcasts. Platforms such as YouTube Live, Facebook Live, and Twitch have become the go-to destinations for live streaming content.

Through live streaming platforms, users gain the ability to engage with content in real-time, employing live chat features and interactive elements. This interactivity fosters a sense of community, enabling viewers to connect with one another and the content creators. Live streaming has rapidly become an indispensable tool for content creators and influencers, facilitating direct engagement with their audience and fostering the growth of a dedicated following.

The rise of social media platforms has ushered in a new category of streaming - social media streaming. Platforms like Instagram Live, Periscope, and Snapchat permit users to stream their own content directly to their social media profiles. This form of streaming has gained traction among individuals and businesses alike, enabling them to share moments, experiences, and announcements in real-time with their followers.

Social media streaming platforms revolve around user-generated content, empowering users to express their creativity and share their unique perspectives with the world. Such platforms often prioritize short-form content and stress the immediacy of the streaming experience. Social media streaming has become an integral part of our daily routines, facilitating our continual connection with friends, family, and the world at large.

Importantly, it is worth noting that the boundaries between these three types of streaming media platforms are not always clearly defined. Many platforms incorporate elements of on-demand, live, and social media streaming into their offerings. For instance, YouTube allows users to stream pre-recorded videos on-demand, as well as live stream events and engage with their audience through comments and likes.

As technology continues to advance, we can anticipate streaming media platforms becoming increasingly diverse and sophisticated. The emergence of virtual reality (VR) and augmented reality (AR) technologies carries immense potential for the future of streaming, allowing users to immerse themselves in virtual worlds and experience content in unprecedented ways.

In conclusion, streaming media presents a vast and ever-evolving landscape. On-demand streaming, live streaming, and social media streaming have each played significant roles in shaping the consumption of audio and video content. Each platform type offers unique features and functionalities, catering to distinct needs and preferences. As a social science researcher, documentary filmmaker, and CEO of a streaming media network, I eagerly anticipate the ongoing growth and innovation within the streaming industry.

The Role of Streaming Media in the Digital Age

Definition and Context:

Streaming media has emerged as a potent medium for delivering audio and video content over the internet, fundamentally transforming the manner in which we consume and produce media. It enables the real-time transmission of data, granting users access to and enjoyment of audio and video content without necessitating its download onto their devices. The dynamic and on-demand nature of streaming media has revolutionized the way in which we encounter entertainment, news, and information.

Advancements in technology, including high-speed internet connectivity, have paved the way for the rapid proliferation and popularity of streaming media. With the increase in smartphones, tablets, and smart TVs, streaming has become an integral component of our daily lives. It has opened up an array of possibilities, affording users instantaneous access to a vast repertoire of content from all corners of the globe.

Cultural Trends:

Streaming media has played a pivotal role in shaping cultural trends in the digital era. It has precipitated the advent of a new epoch in media consumption, challenging traditional media formats and engendering fresh opportunities for content creators. Platforms such as Netflix, Hulu, and YouTube have revolutionized the manner in which we view movies, TV shows, and videos, allowing us to partake in binge-watching entire series or unearthing independent content creators.

The ability to stream content has, additionally, facilitated the globalization of cultural products. In the past, certain forms of media, like foreign films, were confined to limited audiences. With streaming platforms, however, these cultural offerings can now reach a global audience, augmenting cross-cultural understanding and appreciation.

Furthermore, streaming media has fueled the proliferation of niche communities and subcultures. Independent musicians, for instance, can garner popularity by leveraging platforms like Spotify and SoundCloud, accessing audiences that may otherwise have been inaccessible. This democratization of content creation has engendered a diverse range of voices and narratives, thereby enabling a more inclusive representation within the media panorama.

Democratization of Content Creation:

One of the most notable impacts of streaming media in the digital age is the democratization of content creation. It has empowered individuals and organizations with the tools and platforms to generate and disseminate their own audio and video content, devoid of the requirement of expensive equipment or extensive technical expertise.

Platforms such as Twitch and YouTube have endowed individuals with the capability to become content creators, effectively circumventing the gatekeepers of traditional media. Any individual with a smartphone and an internet connection can now share their talents, ideas, and perspectives with a global audience. This phenomenon has not only facilitated the discovery of nascent talent but has also posed a challenge to established media hierarchies, providing a platform for marginalized voices to be heard.

The democratization of content creation has, moreover, revolutionized the business models of the media industry. Through streaming media, content creators can directly monetize their work through advertising, sponsorships, and subscriptions. This disruption of traditional revenue streams has empowered creators to exert greater control over their creative output.

Fostering Global Connectivity:

Streaming media has fostered global connectivity, uniting individuals from all corners of the globe through shared experiences. It has transcended geographic boundaries, enabling people to connect and interact with one another in unprecedented ways.

Platforms such as social media and live streaming services have provided real-time engagement and collaboration, fostering cross-cultural communication and understanding. Live-streamed events, for example, concerts, conferences, and sports matches, can be accessed by individuals across the world, fostering a sense of global community.

Additionally, streaming media has been instrumental in disseminating information, particularly during times of crisis. Live-streamed news coverage allows individuals to remain informed about unfolding events in real-time, irrespective of their location. This accessibility to information has the potential to bridge gaps in knowledge and foster global solidarity.

The Role of Streaming Media in Education and Research:

Streaming media has also permeated into the realm of education and research. Educational institutions have embraced the potential of streaming to enhance teaching and learning experiences. In the digital age, classrooms have expanded beyond their physical confines, with lectures, tutorials, and educational resources being made available online through streaming platforms.

This transition to digital learning has facilitated greater flexibility and accessibility. Students are now able to engage with educational content at their own pace and convenience, regardless of their geographic location. Furthermore, streaming media has facilitated collaborative learning, with students and educators connecting virtually and engaging in real-time discussions.

In the sphere of research, streaming media has presented researchers with new avenues for data collection and analysis. The capacity to stream audio and video content has facilitated qualitative research, enabling the examination of visual and auditory cues that may not be captured through conventional research methodologies. This has enhanced the research process, yielding a more comprehensive understanding of intricate phenomena.

Conclusion:

Streaming media has emerged as a transformative force in the digital age, completely revolutionizing the consumption and production of content. Its dynamic nature has exerted an influence on cultural trends, democratized content creation, fostered global connectivity, and even disrupted education and research.

As technology continues its inexorable evolution, the role of streaming media is poised to expand, further blurring the distinction between traditional and digital media. It is imperative for individuals, organizations, and policymakers to apprehend the significance of streaming media and harness its potential to create a more inclusive, interconnected, and culturally diverse world.

2 |

Chapter 2: Technical Fundamentals of Streaming Media

Streaming Protocols and Standards

One of the most frequently utilized streaming protocols is HTTP Live Streaming (HLS). Developed by Apple, HLS has gained popularity due to its compatibility with various devices and platforms. The protocol segments the media into small files and delivers them to the client via HTTP. This segmentation allows HLS to adapt to varying network conditions, providing a seamless streaming experience to users. Additionally, HLS supports both live and on-demand streaming, making it a versatile choice for broadcasters. However, a disadvantage of HLS is the delay in delivering content, particularly in live streaming scenarios. The segmentation and packaging process can introduce a delay of several seconds, which can be problematic for real-time interactions, such as live sports broadcasts.

Another significant streaming protocol is Dynamic Adaptive Streaming over HTTP (DASH). Unlike HLS, which is proprietary to Apple, DASH is an international standard developed by the Moving Picture Experts Group (MPEG). DASH operates on the principle of adaptive streaming, where the quality of the streamed content adjusts dynamically based on the available network bandwidth. By utilizing a manifest file that contains multiple representations of the media, DASH allows for seamless switching between different quality levels, ensuring an uninterrupted viewing experience for users. This flexibility makes DASH an ideal choice for streaming services that cater to a wide range of devices and network conditions. However, as with HLS, DASH introduces a delay due to the segmentation and packaging process.

One of the earliest streaming protocols that gained popularity in the industry is the Real-Time Messaging Protocol (RTMP). Developed by Macromedia (now Adobe), RTMP has been widely used for live streaming and interactive applications. RTMP utilizes a persistent connection between the client and the server, allowing for real-time communication. This low-latency streaming protocol is particularly suitable for applications where minimal delay is crucial, such as online gaming or live auctions. However, RTMP has lost some of its prominence in recent years due to the rise of newer protocols that offer better compatibility and scalability.

While HLS, DASH, and RTMP are among the most popular streaming protocols, it is essential to mention a few others that have also made an impact in the industry. Microsoft Smooth Streaming, for instance, is a streaming protocol developed by Microsoft that supports adaptive streaming and offers robust DRM support. Smooth Streaming has found its niche in the Microsoft ecosystem, being particularly suitable for streaming to Windows-based devices. Additionally, WebRTC (Web Real-Time Communication) is an open-source project that enables real-time communication in web browsers. Although often associated with video conferencing and peer-to-peer communication, WebRTC can also be used for streaming purposes, allowing for direct interaction between clients and servers.

Every streaming protocol has its own set of strengths and limitations, and selecting the most appropriate one depends on various factors such as the target audience, content type, network conditions, and device compatibility. For instance, HLS and DASH are ideal choices for delivering high-quality video content across different platforms, while

RTMP is more suitable for real-time interactive applications. Additionally, factors such as latency, scalability, and DRM support should also be considered when choosing a streaming protocol.

In conclusion, streaming protocols and standards play a vital role in the audio and video streaming industry. Understanding the nuances of these protocols is crucial for broadcasters, content creators, and streaming service providers. While HLS, DASH, and RTMP are among the most widely used protocols, others like Microsoft Smooth Streaming and WebRTC also offer unique features and functionalities. By selecting the right streaming protocol, content providers can ensure a seamless and optimized streaming experience for their audience. As the industry continues to evolve, it is crucial to stay updated with the latest advancements and trends in streaming protocols and standards to deliver the best possible streaming experience.

Video and Audio Encoding for Streaming

To commence this venture, it is imperative to obtain a fundamental understanding of the concept of encoding. In simpler terms, encoding refers to the process of converting unprocessed audio and video data into a compressed digital format that can be easily transmitted via the internet. The objective is to find an ideal balance between file size and quality to ensure seamless playback for users with varying internet speeds.

One of the essential components of successful streaming is the selection of appropriate codecs, or compression-decompression algorithms, utilized during the encoding process. Codecs play a critical role in reducing file size without compromising quality. Multiple codecs are available in the market, each possessing unique strengths and limitations. Commonly employed codecs for video streaming include H.264, VP9, and AV1, while for audio streaming, AAC, MP3, and Opus are popular choices.

Let us delve deeper into the video encoding process. When encoding video, the initial step is to convert raw video footage into a digital format. This is accomplished by capturing video frames at regular intervals, known as the frame rate, and saving them as individual images. The typical frame rates used in video encoding are 24, 25, and 30 frames per second (fps), although higher frame rates such as 60fps are gaining popularity due to their ability to provide smoother motion.

Once the individual frames are captured, the subsequent step is to compress them using a codec. Compression functions by eliminating redundant information from the frames while retaining crucial details. This reduction in file size is achieved through techniques like spatial compression, temporal compression, and perceptual compression. Spatial compression involves encoding only the variations between consecutive frames, while temporal compression reduces redundancy by encoding only the changes between groups of frames. Perceptual compression exploits human perception limitations to remove less noticeable details, further diminishing file size.

Another pivotal aspect of video encoding is the concept of bitrates. Bitrate pertains to the volume of data transmitted per second and significantly influences the quality of the streamed content. Higher bitrates yield superior image quality but necessitate faster internet connections. Conversely, lower bitrates may result in a decrease in quality but enhance compatibility for users with slower internet speeds. As a streaming provider, striking the right balance between bitrates and user experience is essential, ensuring maximum accessibility without compromising quality.

Equally significant is the selection of resolution during video encoding. Resolution denotes the number of pixels comprising the video frame. Common resolutions encompass standard definition (SD), high definition (HD), and ultra-high definition (UHD). The choice of resolution hinges on factors such as the target audience, the nature of the streamed content and the available internet bandwidth. While higher resolutions like UHD offer breathtaking visuals, they necessitate substantial bandwidth and may exclude users with slower connections.

To optimize the streaming experience, adaptive bitrate streaming (ABR) has gained traction in recent years. ABR dynamically adjusts the quality of the streamed content based on the user's internet connection. It operates by encoding the same video in multiple bitrates and resolutions, seamlessly transitioning between them as conditions change. This methodology guarantees that users with varying internet speeds can enjoy a smooth streaming experience devoid of interruptions or buffering.

As we have expounded upon the intricacies of video encoding, it is crucial to recognize that audio encoding follows a similar process. Nevertheless, audio encoding involves different aspects such as sample rates, bit depths, and audio codecs. Sample rate refers to the number of audio samples recorded per second, with higher sample rates translating to superior audio quality. Conversely, bit depth determines the dynamic range and precision of the audio, with higher bit depths affording more fidelity.

Audio codecs such as AAC, MP3, and Opus employ diverse techniques, including perceptual coding and psychoacoustic modeling, to efficiently compress audio data. Perceptual coding capitalizes on limitations within the human auditory system to eliminate imperceptible details, while psychoacoustic modeling endeavors to predict the hearing threshold for various frequencies and optimize the encoding process accordingly. It is worth noting that choosing the appropriate audio codec is critical to ensure compatibility across diverse devices and platforms.

In conclusion, video and audio encoding for streaming necessitate a delicate balance between file size, quality, and user experience. By employing suitable codecs, bitrates, and resolutions, streaming providers can guarantee that their content is accessible to a wide array of users without compromising on quality. As the Chairman and CEO of a broadcast media streaming network, I comprehend the significance of remaining at the forefront of this ever-evolving field, consistently conducting research, and implementing the best practices to deliver an unparalleled streaming experience to our viewers.

Content Delivery Networks (CDNs)

The smooth and uninterrupted delivery of streamed audio and video content is a crucial aspect of the viewer's experience. Content Delivery Networks, commonly referred to as CDNs, play a vital role in ensuring efficient and reliable content delivery to end-users. CDNs consist of strategically placed network servers worldwide that store and deliver content based on users' geographical locations.

The primary function of a CDN is to reduce latency and enhance content delivery speed. When users request to stream a video or audio file, the CDN identifies their location and directs the request to the closest server in its network. This not only facilitates faster delivery but also reduces the bandwidth necessary on the origin server where the content is stored.

This efficient content delivery system offers several benefits. Firstly, it guarantees a seamless and uninterrupted streaming experience, eliminating the annoyance of waiting for content to load by reducing latency and buffering time. This is particularly critical for live streaming events where viewers expect real-time content without any delays.

Secondly, CDNs can handle heavy traffic loads. In situations where a popular video or audio file goes viral or a live event attracts a large audience, the distributed network of servers within the CDN effectively manages the surge in traffic without compromising the streaming experience for individual users. This scalability is essential for streaming platforms as it allows them to accommodate a growing user base without sacrificing performance.

Additionally, CDNs contribute to cost savings for streaming service providers. By offloading traffic from the origin server to the CDN, providers can reduce bandwidth requirements and minimize the necessity for additional server infrastructure. This not only reduces operational costs but also enhances the overall reliability and availability of the content.

Now that we comprehend the significance and advantages of CDNs, let's explore some popular CDN providers available in the market. It is imperative to select a CDN that aligns with the specific needs and objectives of your streaming service. Each CDN provider has its unique strengths and weaknesses, necessitating a thorough evaluation of their offerings before making a decision.

One of the most well-known CDN providers is Akamai Technologies. With an extensive global network and a strong focus on security and performance, Akamai serves as a dependable choice for numerous streaming platforms. Their comprehensive suite of products includes features like dynamic site acceleration, adaptive media delivery, and security solutions.

Another noteworthy CDN provider is Cloudflare, which offers a robust and highly scalable network with an emphasis on security. With the ability to cache content at the edge, Cloudflare ensures swift and efficient content delivery to users worldwide. They also provide advanced security features such as DDoS protection and web application firewall, which are critical for safeguarding streaming platforms from cyber threats.

Amazon Web Services (AWS) also offers a CDN service called Amazon CloudFront. Making use of the global infrastructure of AWS, CloudFront provides low-latency content delivery with high data transfer speeds. This makes it an enticing option for streaming platforms already utilizing other AWS services, as it seamlessly integrates with the AWS ecosystem.

Other popular CDN providers include Fastly, Limelight Networks, and Verizon Media. Each of these providers offers distinctive features and capabilities, necessitating a thorough evaluation of their offerings and pricing models to determine the best fit for your streaming service.

In conclusion, Content Delivery Networks (CDNs) play an indispensable role in streaming media by ensuring efficient and reliable content delivery to end-users. CDNs contribute to a seamless streaming experience for viewers by reducing latency, handling heavy traffic loads, and offering cost savings. When selecting a CDN provider, factors such as performance, scalability, security, and pricing must be carefully considered. By choosing the appropriate CDN, streaming platforms can efficiently deliver high-quality content to a global audience while maintaining optimal performance and user satisfaction.

Streaming Media Servers

In my capacity as a social science researcher, social entrepreneur, documentary filmmaker, nonprofit executive, and the Chairman and CEO of a broadcast media streaming network, I have had the privilege of firsthand exposure to the transformative capabilities of streaming media servers. These servers play a vital role in the realm of audio and video streaming, facilitating the seamless delivery of content to end-users across a range of devices and platforms.

Let us commence by delving into the fundamentals - what precisely is a streaming media server, and why does it hold such significance?

A streaming media server is a specialized computer system or software that facilitates the transmission of audio and video content over the internet. It serves as an intermediary between the content source, such as a video file, and the end-user, enabling instant playback without having to download the entire file. This technological innovation has ushered in a paradigm shift in the consumption of media, enabling us to enjoy our favorite shows, movies, and music unencumbered by physical media limitations or arduous buffering times.

Multiple types of streaming media servers exist, each offering distinctive functionalities and catering to specific requirements. Allow us to explore some of the most commonly employed ones:

1. Progressive Download Servers:
   a. These servers deliver content by allowing users to download the entire file before playback.
   b. This type of server was widely utilized prior to the advent of true streaming servers and continues to be employed for small-scale applications that do not require real-time streaming.
2. HTTP Streaming Servers:
   a. HTTP streaming servers, also referred to as adaptive streaming servers, utilize the Hypertext Transfer Protocol (HTTP) for content delivery.
   b. They divide media files into smaller segments and dynamically adjust the quality and bitrate based on the user's internet connection, ensuring uninterrupted playback even in the face of fluctuating network conditions.
3. RTSP Streaming Servers:
   a. Real-Time Streaming Protocol (RTSP) servers enable real-time streaming capabilities.
   b. They facilitate the real-time synchronization of audio and video and are commonly employed for live events, video conferencing, and surveillance systems.
4. Media Delivery Platforms:
   a. These platforms merge the capabilities of streaming servers with content management systems, analytics, monetization tools, and other features.
   b. They offer a comprehensive solution for content creators and distributors, enabling efficient delivery, management, and monetization of media assets.

Now that we have gained a better understanding of the various types of streaming media servers, let us delve into the best practices for server setup and management:

1. Scalability:
   a. Establishing a streaming media server necessitates careful consideration of scalability. The server must be able to handle an increasing number of simultaneous connections while maintaining the quality of service.
   b. This can be achieved through load balancing and the distribution of media assets across multiple servers, or via cloud-based solutions that provide elastic scalability.
2. Bandwidth Optimization:
   a. Bandwidth is a precious resource, particularly in the realm of streaming media. Therefore, it is crucial to optimize the server's configuration and network settings to minimize bandwidth consumption while maximizing the quality of the user experience.
   b. Techniques such as adaptive bitrate streaming can be employed to dynamically adjust the content quality based on the user's available bandwidth, ensuring a seamless playback experience for all.
3. Content Distribution:
   a. To ensure widespread availability and minimize latency, it is advisable to geographically distribute streaming servers.
   b. By strategically placing servers in different regions, content can be delivered from the server closest to the end-user, reducing latency and enhancing the overall streaming experience.
4. Monitoring and Analytics:
   a. Server setup and management should encompass robust monitoring and analytics tools to track the performance of the streaming media server.
   b. Real-time monitoring can provide insights into server health, bandwidth usage, and user engagement metrics, enabling proactive troubleshooting and optimization.
5. Security:

a. Security should be of paramount importance when setting up and managing streaming media servers.
b. Implementing strong access controls, encryption, and DRM (Digital Rights Management) technologies can safeguard content from unauthorized access and piracy, preserving its value and integrity.

In conclusion, streaming media servers serve as the backbone of the contemporary digital media landscape, facilitating the seamless delivery of audio and video content to end-users. A comprehensive understanding of the different types of streaming servers, their functionalities, and the implementation of best practices for server setup and management are vital for the establishment of a successful streaming media ecosystem. By harnessing the power of streaming media servers, content creators, distributors, and consumers can unlock new possibilities and enrich their audio and video streaming experiences.

Quality of Service (QoS) in Streaming

The advent of streaming media has revolutionized the consumption of audio and video content, eliminating the need for complete file downloads before enjoying them. The real-time delivery of streaming enables users to instantly access a wide array of audio and video content. Nevertheless, this convenience does not come without challenges.

When it comes to streaming media, Quality of Service (QoS) pertains to the overall performance and reliability of the streaming experience. It encompasses several critical factors, including the speed and consistency of data transfer, the ability to maintain a stable connection, and the avoidance of lag or buffering. Essentially, QoS ensures that the content being streamed reaches the end user in the highest quality and with minimal interruptions. Achieving optimal QoS is imperative for both content creators and consumers as it directly impacts user satisfaction and engagement.

One of the primary factors influencing streaming performance is bandwidth. Bandwidth refers to the maximum amount of data that can be transmitted over a network connection within a specified timeframe. In simpler terms, it serves as the conduit through which data flows from the streaming server to the end user's device. Insufficient bandwidth can result in buffering, interruptions, and an unsatisfactory user experience. Adequate bandwidth is crucial for providing high-quality streaming.

In addition to bandwidth, another essential element that affects QoS is latency. Latency refers to the delay between data transmission from the server and its receipt by the end user's device. High latency can lead to noticeable delays or lag during media streaming, which can be exceptionally frustrating when engaging with real-time or live content. Minimizing latency is vital for maintaining a seamless streaming experience.

Buffering is another factor that impacts QoS. Buffering occurs when the rate at which data is being received by the device is slower than the pace at which it is being played. Consequently, the device pauses playback and waits for additional data to be received before resuming. Buffering is a prevalent issue in streaming media and can be caused by various factors, including a slow internet connection, congested networks, or insufficient processing power. Reducing buffering is critical to ensure uninterrupted playback and a smooth streaming experience.

To optimize QoS, several strategies can be implemented. Firstly, ensuring an adequate and reliable internet connection is paramount. A minimum internet speed of at least 5 Mbps is recommended for standard definition streaming, with higher speeds required for high-definition or 4K streaming. Users on mobile networks should strive for a strong signal strength to maintain a stable connection.

Another strategy to optimize QoS is to employ adaptive streaming techniques. Adaptive streaming adjusts the stream quality in real-time based on available bandwidth and device capability. This ensures that content is delivered at the highest possible quality without buffering or interruptions. By dynamically adapting to network conditions, adaptive streaming allows for a seamless viewing experience, regardless of the user's internet connection.

Closely related to adaptive streaming is the utilization of content delivery networks (CDNs). CDNs consist of geographically distributed servers that efficiently deliver content to users. By caching and hosting content closer to end users, CDNs can reduce latency and improve streaming performance. This distributed approach ensures that users can access content from servers closer to their geographical location, resulting in faster data transfer and reduced buffering.

Lastly, ensuring proper encoding and compression of media files is essential to optimize QoS. This process involves reducing the file size of media content without compromising its quality. By utilizing efficient encoding and compression techniques, the media file's size can be significantly reduced, requiring less bandwidth for streaming. This not only enhances QoS but also reduces the overall load on the network infrastructure.

In conclusion, the maintenance of Quality of Service (QoS) plays a pivotal role in streaming media. By comprehending the factors that impact streaming performance, such as bandwidth, latency, and buffering, content creators and service providers can strive to optimize QoS and provide users with a seamless streaming experience. Strategies such as ensuring adequate bandwidth, minimizing latency, implementing adaptive streaming techniques, utilizing content delivery networks, and optimizing encoding and compression all contribute to enhancing QoS. Continual improvement and innovation in the realm of streaming media will unlock the full potential of audio and video streaming, bringing content closer to users while upholding the highest standards of quality.

Chapter 3: Creating a Streaming Platform

Planning a Streaming Platform

This subchapter outlines the key considerations in planning a streaming platform, including target audience, content strategy, monetization options, and technical requirements. As the Chairman and CEO of a broadcast media streaming network, I have extensively researched and successfully implemented these strategies in my own organization.

Identifying the Target Audience:

When planning a streaming platform, it is imperative to possess a clear comprehension of the target audience. This necessitates conducting extensive market research to discern the demographics, interests, and preferences of the potential viewers. By understanding the needs of the target audience, one can curate content that resonates with them and fosters engagement. For instance, if the platform is focused on educational content for children, the target audience would primarily encompass parents, teachers, and caregivers. Understanding this audience would facilitate the creation of age-appropriate content and user-friendly interfaces.

Crafting a Content Strategy:

Once the target audience is identified, it is time to develop a content strategy that aligns with their interests and needs. An astutely formulated content strategy encompasses a meticulous selection of content genres, formats, and themes that cater to the preferences of the target audience. For example, if the platform is aimed at music enthusiasts, a diverse range of music genres, live performances, and exclusive interviews with artists would be ideal. Additionally, it is crucial to strike a balance between evergreen content and fresh, trending content to ensure continuous engagement.

To develop an effective content strategy, diligent research on current trends and consumer behavior in the streaming industry is indispensable. This entails analyzing popular content on other platforms, identifying market gaps, and conducting surveys or focus groups to acquire direct feedback from the target audience. By amalgamating these insights, one can create a content strategy that is both compelling and sustainable in the long run.

Monetization Options:

Monetization is a pivotal aspect of planning a streaming platform as it delineates the revenue streams and sustainability of the business. There exists a range of monetization options to consider, including subscription-based models, ad-supported models, pay-per-view, and sponsorships. Each option possesses its own advantages and trade-offs. For instance, while a subscription-based model offers recurring revenue and a loyal user base, it may limit the platform's reach to those willing to pay. On the other hand, an ad-supported model provides free access to a larger audience but relies on advertising revenue.

To select the appropriate monetization option, one must take into account factors such as the target audience's willingness to pay, the competitive landscape, and the platform's production costs. Factors like the platform's unique selling points, content quality, and user experience also play an instrumental role in determining the value proposition for potential subscribers or advertisers. It is imperative to strike a balance between generating revenue and providing value to the viewers, thus fostering a mutually beneficial scenario for both the platform and its audience.

Technical Requirements:

In planning a streaming platform, it is vital to address the technical requirements necessary for a smooth and seamless user experience. This encompasses considerations such as video quality, scalability, and compatibility across various devices and internet connections.

To ensure high-quality video streaming, one must invest in robust content delivery networks (CDNs) that can handle the platform's anticipated traffic and deliver content efficiently. It is also imperative to factor in the storage and bandwidth requirements for hosting and streaming the content effectively. Furthermore, compatibility across multiple devices such as smartphones, tablets, smart TVs, and gaming consoles should be prioritized to reach a broader audience.

Apart from technical infrastructure, implementing effective content management systems (CMS) and user interfaces (UI) are crucial for organizing and presenting the content in an intuitive manner. A user-friendly interface not only enhances the viewing experience but also encourages users to explore more content and engage with the platform. Moreover, integrating social media sharing features and interactive elements can further deepen user engagement.

Conclusion:

A meticulously planned streaming platform demands meticulous consideration of the target audience, content strategy, monetization options, and technical requirements. By conducting thorough market research, curating captivating content, selecting the right monetization model, and investing in the necessary technical infrastructure, one can create a successful streaming platform that resonates with the audience and generates revenue. However, it is vital to constantly adapt and refine the platform based on user feedback and changing industry dynamics to stay competitive in the ever-evolving streaming landscape.

Content Acquisition and Licensing

As an experienced professional in the fields of social science research, social entrepreneurship, documentary filmmaking, nonprofit management, and leadership of a broadcast media streaming network, I have dedicated significant time to comprehending the intricacies of content acquisition and licensing for streaming platforms. Within this subchapter, I will provide comprehensive guidance on the process of acquiring and licensing content, encompassing the legal aspects, negotiation strategies, and the critical nature of content curation.

Developing a Comprehensive Grasp of the Legal Aspects

Prior to immersing oneself in the realm of content acquisition, it is imperative to possess a solid understanding of the legal facets associated with this practice. Copyright laws play an integral role in determining the rights and restrictions pertaining to content usage. As a streaming platform, it is essential to navigate copyright laws with the utmost care in order to ensure compliance and sidestep legal complications.

First and foremost, it is advised to familiarize oneself with the doctrine of fair use. The concept of fair use authorizes limited use of copyrighted material without explicit permission from the copyright owner. This is primarily applicable in cases of criticism, commentary, news reporting, teaching, scholarship, or research. Nonetheless, it is crucial to thoroughly apprehend the boundaries of fair use and, if necessary, engage legal experts for guidance.

Furthermore, it is of utmost importance to develop a comprehensive understanding of licensing agreements. These agreements serve as a framework through which the terms and conditions for employing copyrighted content on one's streaming platform are specified. They delineate the scope of usage, duration, distribution channels, and financial arrangements. To safeguard the interests of one's platform, it is indispensable to possess a proficient legal team well-versed in intellectual property law, capable of either drafting or reviewing these agreements.

Researching and Identifying Suitable Content

Once one has acquired a thorough understanding of the legal aspects, it is then time to undertakes the task of researching and identifying the content that one intends to acquire and license for the streaming platform. Carrying out an exhaustive market analysis becomes indispensable for determining the demand and potential audience for specific types of content.

It is advisable to assess the target audience or niche one aims to serve and subsequently identify content that aligns with their interests and preferences. This step calls for meticulous research, encompassing an analysis of trends, conducting surveys, and studying audience behavior. By comprehending the target audience, one can select and curate content that resonates with them, thereby enhancing engagement and promoting user retention on the platform.

Furthermore, it is imperative to consider the importance of diversity and inclusivity in the content one acquires. By presenting a wide range of voices and perspectives, one can create a platform that authentically reflects the diverse world in which we live.

Skillfully Negotiating Content Licenses

Negotiating content licenses necessitates a delicate process that demands a nuanced combination of business acumen and interpersonal skills. When initiating discussions with content owners or distributors, it is crucial to formulate a persuasive pitch that emphasizes the unique selling points of one's streaming platform and justifies why it presents an appealing opportunity for content creators or distributors.

During negotiations, it is vital to be prepared to address financial matters such as royalties, revenue sharing, or flat fees. These discussions should be approached with a clear understanding of budgetary constraints and the potential revenue streams that the platform can generate. It is important to bear in mind that the terms should be mutually beneficial and rewarding for both parties involved.

Additionally, contemplating the provision of promotional opportunities for content creators or distributors can be highly advantageous. By showcasing their work on one's platform, one provides them with exposure and the potential to attract a larger audience. This mutually beneficial relationship contributes to success for all parties involved.

The Significance of Content Curation

Content curation stands as the foundation of a thriving streaming platform. It entails the careful selection, organization, and presentation of content in a manner that enhances the user experience. In order to distinguish oneself in a saturated market, it is essential to curate content that is diverse, of high quality, and aligned with the interests of the user base.

Consideration should be given to creating playlists or collections that cater to specific themes or genres. This approach empowers users to discover new content and fosters engagement and satisfaction. Constantly updating and refreshing the content library enhances the attraction for users, encouraging repeat visits.

Furthermore, data and analytics should be employed in order to inform content curation decisions. Analyzing user behavior, viewing patterns, and feedback provides valuable insights into the content that resonates most with the audience. This data can be harnessed to curate personalized recommendations and improve the discoverability of content on the platform.

Conclusion:

Acquiring and licensing content for a streaming platform is an intricate process that necessitates a comprehensive understanding of the legal aspects, negotiation strategies, and the critical importance of content curation. By adhering to the step-by-step guidance presented within this subchapter, one can successfully navigate the complexities of content acquisition, develop mutually beneficial licensing agreements, and carefully curate a captivating content library for the streaming platform. It remains essential to remain compliant with copyright laws, prioritize diversity and inclusivity, and consistently adapt the content curation approach based on user feedback and data analysis.

Platform Development and Infrastructure

Choosing the appropriate Technology Stack:

Choosing the appropriate technology stack is of utmost importance when it comes to developing a streaming platform. A technology stack refers to the combination of software and programming languages that collaborate to create a functional platform. The selection of a technology stack hinges upon numerous factors, including desired features, target audience, and scalability requisites.

One of the most popular technology stacks for streaming platforms is the LAMP stack, an acronym for Linux, Apache, MySQL, and PHP/Python/Perl. This stack lays a solid foundation for constructing a secure and scalable platform. Nevertheless, there exist alternative stacks such as the MEAN stack (MongoDB, Express, AngularJS, and Node.js) or the MERN stack (MongoDB, Express, ReactJS, and Node.js) that provide both flexibility and performance advantages.

When deciding on a technology stack, it is essential to take into account the expertise of the development team. If the team is already adept in a particular programming language or framework, it may prove beneficial to opt for a stack that aligns with their skill set. Additionally, it is crucial to evaluate the compatibility of the technology stack with other systems intended for integration, such as content delivery networks (CDNs) or analytics platforms.

Scalability Considerations:

Constructing a streaming platform necessitates meticulous consideration of scalability. As the user base expands, the platform must be able to accommodate increased traffic and demand. Failing to account for scalability can result in downtime, slow loading times, and disgruntled users.

Several strategies can be employed to ensure scalability. One such approach is to utilize cloud-based infrastructure, such as Amazon Web Services (AWS) or Microsoft Azure. These platforms offer scalable and flexible infrastructure that can adapt to evolving needs. By leveraging cloud-based solutions, the platform can be easily scaled up or down based on user demand.

Furthermore, integrating a content delivery network (CDN) is another vital consideration. A CDN consists of servers located across varied geographic locations that cache and deliver streaming content. By dispersing the content among numerous servers, a CDN reduces latency and improves the overall streaming experience for users. It also helps relieve the burden on servers during periods of high traffic.

User Experience Design:

An outstanding user experience is critical to the success of a streaming platform. Users anticipate a seamless and intuitive interface that allows for effortless content navigation and consumption. To design an engaging user experience, it is imperative to comprehend the needs and preferences of the target audience.

User research should be initiated to gain insights into the behaviors and expectations of potential users. This can be accomplished through surveys, interviews, and usability testing. By understanding what users desire and require from a streaming platform, the design can be tailored to meet their expectations.

A well-designed user interface (UI) and user experience (UX) can greatly enhance engagement and retention. Factors to be considered include ease of content discovery, intuitive navigation, and customization options. Features such as personalized recommendations, bookmarking, and social sharing can be incorporated to encourage user interaction and retention.

Usability testing forms an integral part of the design process. By observing how users interact with the platform and collecting feedback, pain points and areas requiring improvement can be identified. Design iterations and testing should be based on user feedback to ensure a smooth and enjoyable user experience.

Conclusion:

The development and infrastructure of a streaming platform require careful consideration. Choosing the appropriate technology stack, ensuring scalability, and designing a captivating user experience are critical components that must be taken into account. By following the steps outlined in this section, the path towards creating a robust and engaging streaming platform will be well within reach.

User Interface and Experience

Design Principles:

Effective user interface (UI) and user experience (UX) design require a comprehensive understanding of user behavior and preferences. As a social science researcher, I have conducted numerous studies to uncover insights into user interactions with streaming platforms. One key finding is the significance of simplicity. Users desire a clean and intuitive interface that enables them to easily locate and access desired content. Cluttered layouts with unnecessary elements only serve to confuse and frustrate users, ultimately leading to disengagement.

Another principle to consider is consistency. An inconsistent interface can be disorienting for users, making it challenging for them to navigate and engage with the platform. By employing consistent design elements, such as color schemes, typography, and navigation patterns, users can develop a mental model of how to interact with the platform, thereby enhancing their overall experience.

Additionally, visual hierarchy plays a crucial role in directing user attention. Designers can prioritize important elements and guide users towards their desired actions by utilizing size, color, and placement. For instance, strategically placing a prominent "Play" button in proximity to a video thumbnail can entice users to click and start watching, thus enhancing overall engagement and satisfaction.

Navigation Structures:

The navigation structure of a streaming platform is of paramount importance as it directly influences how users interact with the content. Different platforms employ various navigation patterns, each with its advantages and trade-offs. Some common navigation structures include:

1. Linear Navigation: This structure is straightforward, allowing users to progress through the platform's content in a linear fashion, such as a playlist or a curated series. While linear navigation simplifies the user experience, it may limit users' freedom to explore and customize their viewing preferences.
2. Category-based Navigation: With this structure, content is categorized into genres, themes, or topics, providing users with a menu of options to choose from. Category-based navigation allows for greater customization and personalization as users can select their preferred genres or search for specific topics of interest.
3. Search-based Navigation: Search-based navigation empowers users to find content by entering specific keywords, titles, or names in a search bar. This structure is particularly useful for users seeking specific content or experiencing decision paralysis when faced with an extensive library of options. By providing relevant search results and filters, designers can greatly enhance the user experience.

It is important to note that these navigation structures are not mutually exclusive, and often a combination of them is employed to provide users with a seamless and intuitive browsing experience.

Accessibility Considerations:

Designing for accessibility is an ethical imperative. As a social entrepreneur and documentary filmmaker, I am passionate about creating inclusive experiences that can be accessed by everyone, regardless of their abilities. When it comes to streaming platforms, accessibility considerations are crucial to ensure that individuals with disabilities can also enjoy and engage with the content.

One key aspect to consider is visual accessibility. By providing options for adjustable font sizes, high contrast themes, and compatibility with screen readers, designers can cater to users with visual impairments. Closed captioning is another essential feature for individuals who are deaf or hard of hearing. Additionally, descriptive audio or audio descriptions can be included to aid those with visual impairments in understanding the visual elements of a video.

Furthermore, designing for motor accessibility involves making it easier for individuals with physical disabilities to navigate the platform. This can be achieved through features such as keyboard shortcuts, alternative input methods, and voice commands. By addressing these considerations, designers can create a more inclusive and welcoming streaming environment.

In conclusion, user interface and experience are pivotal aspects of a streaming platform's success. By adhering to design principles such as simplicity, consistency, and visual hierarchy, designers can create an intuitive and engaging interface for users. Various navigation structures, such as linear, category-based, and search-based, can be employed to provide users with seamless browsing experiences. Finally, considering accessibility is essential for ensuring that individuals with disabilities can fully participate in and enjoy the streaming platform. As a social science researcher, social entrepreneur, documentary filmmaker, nonprofit executive, and CEO of a broadcast media streaming network, I am confident that by implementing these principles and considerations, streaming platforms can optimize user satisfaction and create a truly immersive and inclusive experience for all.

Launching and Marketing a Streaming Platform

Strategies for the Pre-Launch Phase:

Prior to the launch of a streaming platform, it is imperative to establish a strong foundation for success. This entails conducting comprehensive market research to identify the target audience and gain insights into their preferences and needs. By attaining a deep understanding of potential viewers, it becomes possible to tailor the platform to their specifications, offering content that resonates with them.

Moreover, creating a detailed business plan that outlines the vision, mission, and goals is essential. This plan will serve as a guiding document, directing decisions and actions throughout the pre-launch phase and beyond. It should also include financial projections, strategic partnerships, and a clear marketing strategy.

Furthermore, building a network of content creators and securing licensing agreements are critical steps during the pre-launch phase. Engaging with talented individuals and negotiating agreements that guarantee a diverse and captivating content library will attract and retain viewers upon the platform's launch.

Tactics for Promotion:

Once the groundwork for the pre-launch phase has been established, it is time to generate excitement and anticipation for the streaming platform. Consider employing the following promotional tactics:

1. Establish a Strong Online Presence: Develop a professional website that showcases the unique features, benefits, and upcoming content of the platform. Optimize it for search engines and

incorporate engaging visuals and compelling copy to attract visitors. Leverage social media platforms to create a buzz, engage with potential viewers, and share regular updates.

2. Launch Teaser Campaigns: Create succinct teasers or trailers that offer viewers a glimpse into the content offerings of the streaming platform. These teasers should be visually captivating and leave viewers eager for more. Release them strategically on social media, video-sharing platforms, and the website to build anticipation prior to the official launch.

3. Collaborate with Influencers: Forge partnerships with social media influencers, bloggers, and industry experts who cater to the target audience. Engage them to produce content that highlights the unique value proposition of the platform and generates buzz. These influencers can leverage their audience base to drive traffic and interest in the streaming platform.

4. Offer Exclusive Pre-Launch Incentives: Reward early adopters and encourage them to spread the word. Provide exclusive discounts, free trials, or access to limited preview content. Encourage these initial users to share positive experiences and recommendations, which will establish credibility and attract additional viewers.

5. Engage with the Media: Reach out to relevant media outlets, both online and offline, to feature the streaming platform. Craft compelling press releases that showcase unique selling points, an exciting content lineup, and any notable partnerships. Media coverage will increase awareness and generate interest among a broader audience.

6. Strategies for Ongoing Audience Engagement:

The launch of a streaming platform is just the beginning of a long-term commitment to engaging and retaining the audience. Employ these strategies to ensure continual audience engagement:

1. Personalize Recommendations: Utilize algorithms and user data to offer personalized recommendations to viewers. Analyze their viewing patterns, interests, and feedback to curate content that aligns with their preferences. By providing tailored suggestions, the viewing experience can be enhanced and viewers are more likely to return to the platform.

2. Host Live Events and Q&A Sessions: Organize live events, virtual premieres, or Q&A sessions with content creators and industry experts. This interactive engagement allows viewers to directly connect with the creators and foster a sense of community. It also provides valuable insights into viewer preferences, aiding in the refinement of content offerings.

3. Organize Social Media Contests and Challenges: Encourage user-generated content and foster engagement by hosting social media contests and challenges. Prompt viewers to share their favorite moments, reviews, or even create their own content using designated hashtags. This generates excitement and extends the reach of the platform as viewers share their experiences with their social networks.

4. Provide Regular Updates and Fresh Content: Keep the platform dynamic and captivate viewers by regularly adding new content and providing updates. This ensures that the audience has more reasons to return to the platform and minimizes the likelihood of them losing interest or seeking alternatives.

5. Establish Customer Support and Encourage Feedback: Establish a responsive customer support system to promptly address any technical issues or inquiries. Encourage viewers to provide feedback and suggestions, actively considering their ideas when feasible. This demonstrates a commitment to customer satisfaction and fosters a sense of loyalty.

In conclusion, launching and marketing a streaming platform necessitates careful planning and a strategic approach. By conducting thorough market research, building a strong online presence, and consistently engaging with the audience, the chances of success can be increased. It is important to remember that the journey does not conclude with the launch – continual audience engagement and adaptation to changing needs are crucial for sustaining and expanding the streaming platform.

Chapter 4: Legal and Copyright Considerations in Streaming

Intellectual Property Rights in Streaming

This subchapter provides an explanation of intellectual property rights within the context of streaming media, encompassing copyrights, trademarks, and patents. It discusses the significance of upholding and safeguarding intellectual property.

As the Chairman and CEO of a broadcast media streaming network, I have consistently held the belief in the power of intellectual property. The capacity to create and safeguard original ideas and content is the driving force behind innovation and progress within the realm of streaming media. Within this subchapter, I will explore the intricacies of intellectual property rights and shed light on the significance of respecting and protecting these rights within the domain of streaming.

Let us begin with copyrights. Copyright protection grants legal rights to creators of original works, such as music, videos, films, and written content, giving them exclusive rights encompassing reproduction, distribution, and performance of their work. Within the context of streaming media, copyrights play a critical role in safeguarding the rights of artists, musicians, filmmakers, and content creators. Streaming platforms must obtain the necessary licenses and permissions to stream copyrighted content, ensuring rightful compensation for creators.

Nevertheless, acquiring these licenses and permissions can be a multifaceted and intricate process. Each country has its distinct copyright laws, necessitating the navigation of a complex legal landscape. As a streaming platform, it is imperative to possess a comprehensive understanding of copyright laws while ensuring compliance in order to evade infringement. Devoting the necessary time to appropriately license and attribute copyrighted content not only safeguards the rights of creators, but also shields streaming platforms from potential legal repercussions.

Furthermore, it is pivotal to educate users on the significance of respecting copyright laws. Streaming platforms have a significant role to play in raising awareness by prominently displaying copyright information and offering resources on the acquisition of proper content licensing. By fostering a culture of respect for intellectual property among users, streaming platforms can contribute to the preservation and promotion of creativity and innovation driving the industry.

Trademarks are another dimension of intellectual property that necessitates consideration within the streaming context. Trademarks safeguard phrases, symbols, designs, or words employed to differentiate and identify goods or services. Within the realm of streaming media, trademarks can encompass brand names, slogans, and logos linked to specific content creators or streaming platforms. Constructing a robust brand and protecting it through trademark registration is crucial for streaming platforms in establishing a distinct identity in a competitive market.

Trademark infringement can arise when a streaming platform or content creator exploits or adopts a trademark similar to an existing one, potentially leading to consumer confusion and dilution of the original brand's distinctiveness, thereby damaging its reputation. Proper trademark research is essential to avoid infringement and ensure that streaming platforms or content maintain their unique identities.

Streaming platforms ought to be proactive in the protection of their trademarks by closely monitoring potential infringements. Leveraging trademark search tools and consulting with legal professionals specializing in intellectual property law can assist in identifying and addressing potential infringements before they evolve into significant problems. Educating employees and content creators on the importance of respecting trademarks is also crucial, as is having policies and guidelines in place to ensure compliance and consistency in branding.

While less commonly associated with streaming media, patents also hold value as a component of intellectual property. Patents protect inventions or unique processes that are novel and not obvious. Within the realm of streaming media, patents can cover technological innovations, such as streaming algorithms, compression techniques, or user interface designs. Obtaining patents can confer a competitive advantage within the industry, safeguarding innovative ideas from being copied or exploited by competitors.

However, the process of acquiring patents and navigating through the patent system can prove to be complex and costly. As a streaming platform, it is essential to evaluate the advantages and costs of pursuing patents for technological innovations. Seeking guidance and assistance from intellectual property attorneys specializing in patents can provide valuable insights into determining whether patent protection is a worthwhile pursuit.

Respecting and protecting intellectual property rights should be a priority for streaming platforms and content creators. In addition to legal and ethical considerations, upholding intellectual property promotes a healthy and sustainable streaming industry. It engenders innovation, rewards creativity, and fosters an environment conducive to the flourishing of original ideas.

In conclusion, intellectual property rights hold a crucial position in the realm of streaming media. Copyrights, trademarks, and patents all serve to safeguard the rights of creators and cultivate a culture of creativity and innovation. Streaming platforms must be diligent in obtaining the requisite licenses and permissions for copyrighted content, protecting their trademarks, and determining whether patent protection is necessary for their technological innovations. By respecting and protecting intellectual property, streaming platforms can contribute to the industry's growth and sustainability, whilst ensuring rightful acknowledgment and compensation for creators.

Licensing Agreements for Streaming Platforms

As an experienced social science researcher and CEO of a broadcast media streaming network, I have dedicated extensive time to the study and navigation of intricate licensing agreements within streaming platforms. In the following subchapter, I will share my specialized insights and expertise on this topic, shedding light on the various agreement types and the legal complexities surrounding them.

The streaming media industry has experienced substantial growth in recent years, with dominant platforms such as Netflix, Spotify, and YouTube. However, the success of these platforms heavily relies on their ability to obtain the necessary licenses to stream copyrighted content. Content licensing serves as the foundation upon which the streaming industry operates.

Content licensing agreements establish contracts between streaming platforms and content owners, granting the platforms the rights to stream their content. These agreements can significantly differ in terms of scope, duration, and financial arrangements. Typically, streaming platforms compensate content owners with a licensing fee in exchange for the rights to distribute their content to a extensive audience.

Negotiating content licensing agreements is a complex process that necessitates thorough consideration of various factors. The initial step involves identifying the desired content and determining the necessary streaming rights. Once identified, the negotiation process commences through discussions encompassing the scope of the agreement, territorial restrictions, duration, and exclusivity. Content owners often retain the right to simultaneously stream their content through other channels or impose specific platform restrictions.

Another crucial aspect of content licensing agreements is the establishment of financial terms. Generally, streaming platforms and content owners negotiate revenue-sharing models, wherein royalties are paid to content owners based on the number of streams or subscribers. The negotiation of royalty rates can prove challenging, as both parties strive to achieve a delicate balance between fair compensation for content owners and sustainable profitability for the streaming platform.

Performance rights agreements serve as an integral element of licensing agreements within the streaming media industry. These agreements involve obtaining the rights to publicly perform copyrighted music or other audio content. Streaming platforms commonly require performance rights agreements with music publishers and collecting societies to ensure lawful streaming of copyrighted music to their users.

Performance rights agreements are often intricate due to the multitude of stakeholders involved. Negotiations may involve discussions with multiple music publishers, songwriters, and artist representatives, each holding a vested interest in their intellectual property. For streaming platforms, extensive due diligence is essential in order to secure the appropriate rights and permissions to legally stream copyrighted music.

Compensation in the form of royalty payments constitutes a crucial component of performance rights agreements. Streaming platforms bear the responsibility of compensating copyright holders, typically through the payment of royalties based on the number of streams or a percentage of revenue generated from music streaming. The challenge lies in accurately tracking and reporting the usage of copyrighted material and ensuring that the rightful stakeholders receive the appropriate royalties.

In addition to content licensing and performance rights agreements, streaming platforms must also consider the legal and financial implications of music licensing. Music licensing agreements involve securing the rights to use copyrighted music in audiovisual content such as films, TV shows, or commercials. Negotiations for these agreements often encompass discussions with music labels, publishers, and individual artists who hold the rights to their compositions.

When negotiating music licensing agreements, streaming platforms must carefully consider factors such as synchronization rights, enabling the combination of music with visual elements, and mechanical rights, pertaining to the reproduction and distribution of the music. Moreover, the desired duration and scope of the license must be meticulously defined to ensure compliance with copyright laws.

Implementing licensing agreements within the streaming media industry involves not only negotiating and signing contracts but also streamlining processes for reporting and royalty tracking. Streaming platforms must establish robust systems to accurately track and report the usage of copyrighted content, guaranteeing that the appropriate royalties are paid to content owners.

Technological solutions such as digital rights management (DRM) systems, content identification tools, and data analytics platforms play a pivotal role in the effective implementation of licensing agreements. These tools enable streaming platforms to identify and track copyrighted content, monitor its usage, and generate reports facilitating royalty calculations and payments.

In conclusion, licensing agreements constitute a fundamental aspect of the streaming media industry. Content licensing, performance rights agreements, and music licensing all require meticulous negotiation and consideration of legal complexities. It is essential for streaming platforms to navigate these intricacies in order to ensure compliance with copyright laws, secure the necessary rights, and establish fair compensation structures for content creators. Through a comprehensive understanding of the various types of licensing agreements and the legal considerations they entail, streaming platforms can prosper within the dynamic and ever-evolving streaming media industry.

Digital Rights Management (DRM)

As the Chairman and CEO of a broadcast media streaming network, I have always prioritized the safeguarding of copyrighted material and the provision of a top-notch user experience for our customers. To achieve these objectives, Digital Rights Management (DRM) technology plays an indispensable role.

DRM technology comprises a set of security measures and protocols designed to safeguard digital content from unauthorized use and distribution. It empowers content owners to control how their content is accessed, consumed, and shared by users. The absence of DRM would render streaming platforms susceptible to piracy, which in turn could have detrimental effects on the revenue streams of content creators and distributors.

Today, there are numerous DRM technologies available in the market, each having its own set of strengths and weaknesses. Some of the most frequently employed DRM technologies include Apple FairPlay, Microsoft PlayReady, and Google Widevine.

Apple FairPlay is the DRM technology employed by Apple in its digital media services, including iTunes and Apple Music. It affords robust protection for copyrighted content while ensuring that only authorized users can access and utilize said content. FairPlay leverages encryption to safeguard media files and employs a secure playback protocol to prevent unauthorized copying and redistribution.

Conversely, Microsoft PlayReady serves as the DRM technology utilized by Microsoft in its streaming media services, such as Netflix and Hulu. PlayReady offers comparable levels of content protection as FairPlay while additionally being compatible with a wide array of devices and platforms. This makes it a popular choice among content providers desiring to reach a broad audience.

Google Widevine is another widely adopted DRM technology used by various streaming platforms, including YouTube and Amazon Prime Video. Recognized for its versatility and broad device compatibility, Widevine supports different tiers of content protection, enabling content providers to select the level of security best aligned with their requirements.

While DRM technologies are vital for preserving copyrighted content, they can also influence the user experience. For instance, DRM often necessitates user authentication of devices or the installation of software plugins to decrypt protected content. This supplementary step can prove vexing for certain users, particularly those utilizing less common devices or operating systems.

To address these concerns, streaming platforms and device manufacturers are continuously working to enhance the user experience by seamlessly integrating DRM technologies. Many devices now come pre-installed with the requisite DRM components, sparing users from the need to install supplementary software. Additionally, streaming platforms are employing adaptive streaming technologies that can dynamically adjust video quality and resolution based on the user's device capacities and internet connection speed. This ensures that users can enjoy smooth playback experiences, regardless of the specific DRM technology in use.

While DRM technologies have been successful in shielding copyrighted content, they are not infallible. Instances have arisen in which DRM systems have been circumvented, enabling unauthorized access to protected content. Content creators and streaming platforms must remain vigilant and stay abreast of the latest developments in DRM technologies and vulnerabilities to ensure the highest possible level of content security.

In conclusion, Digital Rights Management (DRM) serves as a vital element of the streaming media industry. It enables content owners and distributors to safeguard their copyrighted material from unauthorized use and piracy. While DRM technologies invariably impact the user experience, progress in the field is steadily advancing the integration and compatibility of DRM systems. By staying well-informed regarding the latest technologies and vulnerabilities, content creators and streaming platforms can guarantee the security and integrity of their digital content.

Privacy and Data Protection

The recent advancements in technology have significantly transformed the media consumption landscape, with increasing popularity of streaming platforms. However, alongside this convenience, it is imperative to address the privacy concerns that arise from the collection and utilization of user data. In the realm of streaming media, user data is commonly collected through various methods, such as cookies, IP addresses, and user profiles. Subsequently, this data is analyzed and utilized to personalize the user experience, target advertisements, and gain insights into user preferences.

Streaming platforms have a legal responsibility to comply with frameworks governing the protection of user data, for example, the General Data Protection Regulation (GDPR) in the European Union and the California Consumer Privacy Act (CCPA) in the United States. These regulations mandate that streaming platforms obtain user consent before collecting and utilizing their data, offer transparency in data collection practices, and empower users to exercise control over their personal information. Failure to abide by these regulations can result in severe penalties and harm to the platform's reputation.

To ensure the privacy and data protection of users, streaming platforms should implement a range of measures. A crucial step is to encrypt user data, safeguarding it against unauthorized access. Encryption guarantees that in the event of a breach, the data becomes incomprehensible to individuals without the appropriate encryption key. Furthermore, platforms should establish strong access controls and authentication mechanisms to restrict access to sensitive user data solely to authorized individuals.

Another essential aspect of privacy protection within streaming media is the responsible usage and storage of user data. Streaming platforms should have clear policies on data retention, stipulating the duration for which user data will be retained. By minimizing the retention period, platforms can reduce the risk of data breaches and unauthorized access. In addition, platforms should conduct regular audits and assessments to ensure compliance with privacy regulations and to identify any potential vulnerabilities in their systems.

To foster trust with users, streaming platforms should be transparent regarding their data collection practices and the purposes for which user data is utilized. Privacy policies should comprehensively outline the types of data that are collected, how it is stored, and how it is used. Moreover, platforms should offer users the ability to exercise control over their data, such as opting out of targeted advertising or deleting personal information.

Furthermore, it is crucial for streaming platforms to obtain explicit user consent before collecting any sensitive data, such as financial information or health data. This ensures that users are fully aware of the collection and usage of their data and have the autonomy to share or withhold sensitive information as they see fit.

In addition to legal and technical measures, streaming platforms should also adopt ethical best practices pertaining to privacy and data protection. This includes respecting user privacy preferences and ensuring that data is used in a responsible and ethical manner. It is vital for platforms to prioritize user privacy over monetization and to handle user data with utmost care and respect.

In conclusion, privacy and data protection are of paramount importance in the realm of streaming media. Streaming platforms must be conscious of and compliant with legal frameworks such as the GDPR and CCPA to guarantee the responsible collection, storage, and utilization of user data. Through the implementation of encryption, access controls, and clear data retention policies, platforms can mitigate the risk of data breaches and unauthorized access. Transparency and user control are also pivotal, as platforms should transparently communicate their data collection practices and empower users to manage their data. Ultimately, the responsible and ethical use of user data should serve as the guiding principle for streaming platforms, ensuring the safeguarding of user privacy and fostering trust among their users.

Compliance and Regulatory Obligations

One of the most crucial compliance obligations that streaming platforms must address is the implementation of age restrictions. The accessibility and convenience of streaming media have contributed to its widespread popularity across various age groups. However, it is important to acknowledge that certain content may not be suitable for all age groups. Therefore, streaming platforms are required to establish age verification mechanisms to ensure that minors are protected from accessing inappropriate content. Age verification processes can include simple checkbox acknowledgments or more sophisticated methods, such as requiring credit card information or linking accounts to social media profiles. Crafting a comprehensive age restriction policy is essential to avoid legal repercussions and maintain a safe environment for our users.

Another significant aspect of compliance in the realm of streaming media is content labeling. Similar to traditional media, streaming platforms must accurately and informatively label their content. This allows viewers to make informed decisions regarding what they are about to watch. Content rating systems, such as the well-recognized Motion Picture Association (MPA) rating system, can serve as a helpful reference for streaming platforms. These systems categorize content based on criteria such as violence, sexual content, and language, and assign appropriate ratings such as G, PG, or R. Implementing a content labeling system not only ensures compliance with regulations but also enhances user experience by enabling viewers to find content that aligns with their preferences.

In addition to age restrictions and content labeling, streaming platforms must also address accessibility requirements. Accessibility is not merely a legal obligation but also a moral responsibility. Ensuring that individuals with disabilities can access and enjoy streaming content is crucial for creating an inclusive platform. Making streaming media accessible entails providing closed captions for the deaf or hard of hearing, audio descriptions for the visually impaired, and options for adjusting font sizes and color contrasts. As the Chairman and CEO, I am committed to surpassing the minimum legal requirements to ensure our platform's accessibility to as many individuals as possible.

Apart from these obligations, streaming platforms may have other compliance requirements based on the nature of their content. For instance, if a platform hosts copyrighted material or permits user-generated content, it must address concerns related to copyright infringement and establish a robust content moderation system. The Digital Millennium Copyright Act (DMCA) in the United States provides a legal framework for addressing online copyright infringement and offers a safe harbor for platforms that promptly respond to takedown notices.

Moreover, privacy and data protection are significant concerns for streaming platforms due to the extensive personal information they collect from users. Complying with data protection laws, such as the General Data Protection Regulation (GDPR) in the European Union, is vital for maintaining user trust and safeguarding their privacy. Implementing robust data security measures and providing clear communication of privacy policies to users are essential steps in meeting these compliance obligations.

It is crucial for streaming platforms to recognize that compliance and regulatory obligations are not trivial bureaucratic responsibilities. Rather, they serve as the foundation for a trustworthy and reliable platform. By adhering to these obligations, platforms can ensure the safety, privacy, and overall satisfaction of their users. Furthermore, legal compliance can facilitate stronger partnerships with content creators, advertisers, and other industry stakeholders for streaming platforms.

As the Chairman and CEO of our broadcast media streaming network, I am fully aware of the importance of staying informed about the ever-changing compliance landscape. New laws and regulations are continuously introduced to address emerging issues in the streaming media industry. Therefore, conducting regular audits, seeking legal advice, and monitoring industry updates are practices that we must adopt to stay ahead of compliance obligations.

In conclusion, compliance and regulatory obligations play a pivotal role in the success of streaming platforms. Age restrictions, content labeling, accessibility requirements, copyright infringement, data protection, and privacy are some of the key areas that streaming platforms must prioritize. Through a commitment to legal compliance, our broadcast media streaming network will establish trust among its users and position itself as a responsible and ethical participant in the industry. As the Chairman and CEO, I am devoted to leading our network on the path of legal compliance and upholding the highest standards in the streaming media landscape.

Chapter 5: Monetization Strategies for Streaming Platforms

Subscription Models

The freemium model is a common subscription model utilized by streaming platforms. This model offers users both free and paid options, providing limited access to content for free and requiring a subscription fee for additional features or a wider range of content. The freemium model allows streaming platforms to attract a larger user base and allows users to try the service before committing to a paid subscription.

The freemium model has clear advantages. By offering free access to some content, streaming platforms can build a diverse and large user community, which serves as a valuable marketing tool. Satisfied free users are more likely to recommend the platform to others. The free tier also allows streaming platforms to collect data on user behavior and preferences, which can help improve the service and target advertising. Furthermore, the freemium model can address customers' concerns about paying for a service they have not yet experienced.

However, the freemium model also presents challenges. Streaming platforms must bear the cost of server bandwidth and provisioning additional content for free access, which can be expensive. Moreover, the free tier may cannibalize revenue from paid subscriptions as some users may be content with the limited free access and not upgrade.

To mitigate these challenges, streaming platforms often implement customer retention strategies when using the freemium model. Time-limited trials of premium features are commonly used to entice free users to upgrade, as well as offering exclusive content or early access to new releases as incentives for paid subscriptions. Personalized recommendations and a seamless user experience are also important for keeping users engaged and eager to upgrade.

Another popular subscription model is the tiered pricing model, where streaming platforms offer different levels of service at varying price points. Each tier provides access to specific features or content, with higher-priced tiers offering more benefits. The objective of this model is to offer users options tailored to their needs and budget, while generating additional revenue from higher-tier subscriptions.

The tiered pricing model has advantages for both streaming platforms and users. It allows platforms to have flexibility in pricing and revenue generation, while users can choose a subscription that aligns with their interests and usage patterns. Those who desire a broader range of content or premium features can opt for a higher-tier subscription, while more casual users may find a lower-tier option sufficient. This model also provides opportunities for upselling, as platforms can offer promotions to encourage users to upgrade to higher tiers.

However, the tiered pricing model also faces challenges. Complex pricing structures can confuse potential subscribers and deter them from committing to a paid subscription. Striking the right balance between the features offered at each tier can be difficult, as offering too few features in lower tiers may not provide enough incentive for users to upgrade, while offering too many features may discourage users from subscribing to higher tiers. Finding the sweet spot that satisfies both platforms and users is essential for successful implementation of the tiered pricing model.

To overcome these challenges, streaming platforms using the tiered pricing model often rely on data and analytics. By analyzing user behavior and preferences, platforms can better tailor their tiered offerings to what their users want. Additionally, user feedback and surveys provide valuable insights for improving or adjusting the tiers to meet user expectations. Regular communication with subscribers, through means such as email newsletters or personalized notifications, helps platforms convey the value of each tier and encourage upgrades.

The bundled services model is another subscription pricing approach gaining popularity. In this model, streaming platforms bundle their services with other related products or services, often from partner companies. This adds value to subscribers and sets the platform apart from competitors. Bundled services can include combining a video streaming service with a music streaming service or offering discounts on third-party products or services to subscribers.

The bundled services model has multifaceted advantages. For streaming platforms, it allows diversification and expansion into new markets by leveraging existing customer bases and cross-promotion opportunities through partnerships. Bundling services increases the perceived value for subscribers, as they receive more for their money. Furthermore, this model encourages customer loyalty, as it becomes more inconvenient for subscribers to cancel multiple services or switch providers.

Effective implementation of the bundled services model requires careful consideration and planning. Streaming platforms must ensure that bundled offerings are relevant and complementary to their core services. Partner companies involved must align with the platform's values and target audience. Communication and collaboration with partners are crucial to avoid confusion and create a seamless customer experience. Striking the right balance between the benefits offered through partnerships and potential challenges, such as revenue sharing or customer support management, is essential.

Customer retention remains a central focus for streaming platforms using the bundled services model. Platforms often provide exclusive discounts or special offers for bundled subscribers to incentivize them to stay subscribed. By continuously expanding and refreshing bundled offerings, platforms can keep subscribers engaged and prevent churn. Leveraging data and analytics to understand subscriber behavior and preferences can also inform content curation and personalized recommendations, further enhancing the user experience.

In conclusion, subscription models are crucial for the sustainability and success of streaming platforms. The freemium model, tiered pricing model, and bundled services model are three approaches tailored to different objectives and diverse user needs. Each model offers distinct advantages and challenges, and streaming platforms must carefully consider their target audience, content offering, and strategic partnerships when selecting the most appropriate model. By implementing effective customer retention strategies and leveraging data-driven insights, streaming platforms can maximize revenue generation and create long-lasting relationships with their subscribers.

Advertising and Sponsorship

Advertising and sponsorship are pivotal to the success of streaming platforms. As the Chairman and CEO of a broadcast media streaming network, I have personally witnessed the importance of effective advertising strategies in generating revenue and sustaining the growth of our platform. In this section, we will delve into the various aspects of advertising and sponsorship in the world of streaming media, exploring different formats, programmatic advertising, brand partnerships, and the challenges that arise when trying to balance user experience with revenue generation.

Let us begin by examining the various advertising formats commonly used in streaming platforms. Traditional pre-roll, mid-roll, and post-roll advertisements, which have long been prevalent in television advertising, have also made their way into online streaming. These formats involve placing advertisements either before, during, or after the content that users are streaming. While these formats may effectively reach a large audience, they can also intrude and disrupt the viewing experience. Thus, it is crucial for streaming platforms to carefully consider the placement and frequency of these advertisements to avoid alienating users.

Another popular advertising format in the streaming world is native advertising. This involves seamlessly integrating ads into the content itself, creating a more organic and less disruptive advertising experience for viewers. Native ads can take the form of product placements, sponsored content, or even branded storylines within the streamed content. This type of advertising can be highly effective as it blends seamlessly with the overall user experience. However, it also raises ethical concerns regarding transparency and the potential for deceptive marketing practices. Streaming platforms must strike a delicate balance between monetization and maintaining the trust of their users.

In recent years, programmatic advertising has gained momentum in the world of streaming media. Programmatic advertising involves the use of algorithms and real-time data to automate the buying and selling of ad inventory. This enables advertisers to deliver targeted ads to specific audiences based on demographics, behavior, and other factors. Programmatic advertising can be more efficient and cost-effective for advertisers. However, it can also result in an increase in the number of advertisements users are exposed to, potentially diminishing the overall user experience. Therefore, streaming platforms must carefully implement programmatic advertising strategies while ensuring that user satisfaction remains a top priority.

Aside from traditional advertising methods, brand partnerships have become an increasingly popular avenue for monetizing streaming platforms. Brand partnerships involve collaborating with well-known brands to develop co-branded content or exclusive sponsorship deals. These partnerships provide a new revenue stream for streaming platforms and enhance the overall user experience by offering value-added content or exclusive access to certain features. However, streaming platforms must be cautious when entering into brand partnerships, as they need to maintain their independence and credibility while delivering an authentic experience for their users.

Balancing user experience and revenue generation is an ongoing challenge in the world of streaming media. Streaming platforms need to generate revenue to sustain their operations and deliver high-quality content to users. However, they must prioritize the user experience to retain and attract viewers. Achieving the right balance requires careful planning, continuous evaluation, and a willingness to adapt and innovate. User feedback and engagement play a critical role in guiding the development of advertising strategies that align with user preferences and expectations.

In conclusion, advertising and sponsorship are integral to the monetization of streaming platforms. The various advertising formats, programmatic advertising, brand partnerships, and the challenges of balancing user experience and revenue generation all play a significant role in shaping the advertising landscape of streaming media. As the Chairman and CEO of a broadcast media streaming network, I have learned that successful advertising strategies are those that enhance the user experience, provide value to advertisers, and maintain the trust and satisfaction of the users. By carefully considering these factors and adapting to the ever-evolving landscape of streaming media, streaming platforms can maximize their monetization potential while delivering a seamless and enjoyable experience for their viewers.

Pay-Per-View and Transactional Models

The pay-per-view model, also referred to as the rental model, is a system whereby viewers pay a fee in order to access specific content for a limited duration of time. This particular model has gained widespread popularity in the film industry, allowing individuals to rent and stream movies from the comfort of their own homes. Nevertheless, pay-per-view extends beyond movies and can also be employed for live events, concerts, sports matches, and educational seminars.

One of the primary benefits of the pay-per-view model lies in its flexibility. Viewers have the liberty to select the content they desire to stream without any obligations to long-term commitments or subscriptions. This aspect not only serves individuals who wish to watch a specific movie or event without the hassle of monthly payments, but it also offers content creators, specifically independent filmmakers and small production companies, an opportunity to monetize their work based on the number of views.

Furthermore, the pay-per-view model fosters the democratization of content distribution. Previously, premium content could only be accessed through theaters, television broadcasts, or physical media such as DVDs. However, with the advent of streaming technology, content creators can now reach a global audience without the need for costly physical distribution infrastructure. This accessibility has revolutionized the industry, empowering innovative filmmakers and performers to showcase their work to a wider audience while granting viewers greater choices in terms of the content they consume.

However, it is important to acknowledge the limitations of the pay-per-view model. One of the main drawbacks is the absence of ownership. Unlike the purchase of a physical copy of a movie or album, the pay-per-view model only provides temporary access to the content for a specific period of time. This can be problematic for certain viewers who wish to possess a permanent copy of their favorite films or shows. Additionally, the cost of repeated rentals can accumulate, making it more economically feasible for frequent viewers to opt for subscription-based streaming services instead.

Conversely, the transactional model offers an alternative approach to accessing content within the streaming media landscape. In this model, viewers have the option to purchase and own the desired content, allowing them to watch it repeatedly at their leisure without any time restrictions. The transactional model is commonly used for movies, TV show seasons, music albums, and digital books, and has gained popularity due to its convenience and permanence.

The transactional model provides viewers with a sense of ownership and control over their media collection. By purchasing content, viewers have the freedom to watch or listen to it whenever and wherever they choose, even if their subscription to a streaming platform expires. In addition, content creators benefit from this model since they receive a higher share of revenue compared to the pay-per-view model. This incentivizes established and emerging artists alike to continue producing high-quality content, knowing that their work can be directly purchased by their supporters.

Nevertheless, similar to any model, the transactional model also possesses its own drawbacks. The upfront cost of purchasing individual pieces of content can serve as a barrier for some viewers, particularly those who are accustomed to the convenience of subscription-based services. The transactional model also necessitates viewers to commit to specific content, which may limit their exposure to new or unfamiliar content. Furthermore, the responsibility of managing and organizing a digital media collection falls on the viewer, which can be overwhelming for individuals with extensive libraries or technical challenges.

When examining the relevance of these models across different content genres, it is crucial to recognize that each genre possesses its own distinct characteristics and audience preferences. For instance, in the realm of movies, the pay-per-view model offers filmmakers the opportunity to simultaneously release their films in theaters and on streaming platforms, thus expanding their reach to a wider audience. With regards to live events, such as concerts or sports matches, the pay-per-view model enables fans to enjoy the excitement and energy of the event from the comfort of their own homes.

Conversely, the transactional model may be better suited for genres in which repeat viewings are common, such as TV shows and music albums. Fans of a particular TV show often desire to rewatch favorite episodes or binge-watch entire seasons, making the transactional model a more financially manageable choice in the long run. Similarly, music enthusiasts who enjoy listening to an album on repeat may prefer owning a digital copy rather than paying for each individual play.

In conclusion, the pay-per-view and transactional models hold significant relevance in the realm of streaming media. They provide viewers with the flexibility to choose what they wish to watch without being tied to long-term subscriptions, while also providing content creators with opportunities to monetize their work on a per-view or per-purchase basis. Understanding the advantages and disadvantages of these models, as well as their suitability within different content genres, is crucial for both viewers and content creators to navigate the ever-evolving landscape of streaming media.

Merchandise Sales and E-commerce Integration

As an individual with experience as a social science researcher, social entrepreneur, documentary filmmaker, nonprofit executive, and the Chairman and CEO of a broadcast media streaming network, I have always been dedicated to maximizing revenue opportunities. The realm of streaming media presents countless possibilities, with merchandise sales and e-commerce integration being two avenues that hold immense potential.

Merchandise sales have long been a staple in traditional media, as enthusiasts of favorite bands, movies, or television shows eagerly purchase t-shirts, posters, and other items to show their support. However, within the world of streaming media, the opportunities are even greater. With a global audience at one's fingertips, the potential for merchandise sales is virtually boundless.

When it comes to merchandise sales on streaming platforms, product licensing is a critical aspect. By obtaining licensing agreements with popular brands, artists, or franchises, streaming platforms can tap into a pre-established fan base. These agreements allow for the creation and sale of merchandise that resonates with viewers while providing an additional source of revenue.

Successful product licensing hinges on understanding the preferences and values of the audience. Extensive research plays a vital role in identifying the types of products that would be most enticing to viewers. Is the majority of the audience comprised of music lovers, film enthusiasts, or gamers? Understanding these interests and aligning merchandise offerings accordingly will enhance the likelihood of sales.

Merchandising strategies are equally vital in generating revenue from merchandise sales. The initial step involves creating visually appealing and high-quality products that fans will take pride in wearing or displaying. Collaboration with skilled designers and artists can guarantee aesthetically pleasing merchandise that also aligns with the brand identity. Offering a diverse range of products, such as clothing, accessories, and collectibles, allows streaming platforms to cater to varying tastes and preferences, further increasing the likelihood of sales.

Another successful merchandising strategy involves limited edition releases. By fostering a sense of exclusivity and scarcity, streaming platforms can generate excitement and urgency among fans. Limited edition merchandise often becomes highly sought after, driving up demand and resulting in higher sales. This strategy is particularly effective when utilized in conjunction with special events or milestones, such as the release of a highly anticipated film or the celebration of a streaming platform anniversary.

The subsequent crucial step in monetizing merchandise sales involves e-commerce integration. Streaming platforms should strive to establish a seamless online shopping experience for viewers. This entails integrating an e-commerce platform directly into the streaming website or app, allowing viewers to browse and purchase merchandise without leaving the platform. This not only enhances convenience for customers but also increases the chances of impulse purchases. Streamlining the purchasing process and offering secure payment options can foster trust and encourage repeat business.

The importance of brand synergy cannot be overemphasized in terms of merchandise sales and e-commerce integration. Streaming platforms must ensure that their merchandise aligns with their brand identity and values. Remaining authentic and true to their core mission allows platforms to forge a strong connection with their audience. This connection, in turn, will drive demand for merchandise and increase the likelihood of repeat purchases.

Furthermore, partnering with like-minded brands or influencers can help amplify the reach and impact of merchandise sales. Collaborating with brands or individuals that share similar values and target similar audiences allows streaming platforms to tap into new markets and attract new customers. Cross-promotion through social media, joint events, or exclusive deals can prove mutually beneficial and significantly boost merchandise sales.

To fully harness the potential of merchandise sales and e-commerce integration, streaming platforms must constantly assess and adapt their strategies. Regular analysis of sales data, customer feedback, and market trends can yield valuable insights into what is working and what requires improvement. This data-driven approach allows platforms to optimize their merchandise offerings and marketing efforts, maximizing revenue potential.

In conclusion, merchandise sales and e-commerce integration present immense opportunities for streaming platforms to diversify their revenue streams. Through product licensing, merchandising strategies, and a focus on brand synergy, platforms can tap into the enthusiasm and loyalty of their audience. By creating visually appealing and high-quality merchandise, integrating e-commerce platforms into their streaming websites or apps, and continuously assessing and adapting their strategies, streaming platforms can create a lucrative ecosystem that benefits both the platform and its viewers. Merchandise sales and e-commerce integration are not merely revenue sources; they are an extension of the streaming experience, allowing viewers to express their fandom and support in tangible and meaningful ways.

Analytics and Data-Driven Monetization

In the fast-evolving realm of streaming media, the utilization of analytics and data-driven decision-making is of utmost importance in the achievement of success for online platforms. As the Chairman and CEO of a broadcast media streaming network, I have actively observed and participated in the merging of technology and media. Through my experiences as a social science researcher, I have come to appreciate the immense power that data holds in comprehending user behavior and creating personalized experiences.

Foremost, it is crucial to establish a clear comprehension of analytics. In the context of streaming media, analytics refers to the collection, measurement, analysis, and interpretation of data for the purpose of informed decision making. This encompasses the gathering of extensive data points - from user demographics and viewing habits to engagement and interaction metrics - with the aim of gaining actionable insights.

The significance of data in the monetization of streaming platforms lies in its ability to inform content strategy, target advertising, and optimize user experiences. By leveraging user data, streaming platforms are able to ascertain the type of content that resonates with their audience and subsequently tailor their offerings accordingly. For instance, a music streaming service may utilize data on user listening preferences to recommend personalized playlists or suggest similar artists. This not only enhances user satisfaction but also increases the probability of engagement and, ultimately, monetization.

Personalization is a pivotal aspect of data-driven monetization strategies. These strategies utilize user data to create unique and relevant experiences for individuals. This can be achieved through content recommendations, targeted advertising, or even curated playlists. By employing algorithms to examine user behavior, streaming platforms can provide users with content that aligns with their interests, leading to heightened engagement and potential revenue streams.

However, the use of user data for personalization necessitates careful consideration of ethical implications. As streaming platforms accumulate increasing amounts of user data, concerns pertaining to privacy and data security arise. It is essential for platform operators to protect user information and acquire explicit consent for data collection and usage. Prioritizing transparency and accountability in data-driven monetization strategies ensures the preservation of user trust.

To address these concerns, industry standards and regulations have been established. Organizations such as the Interactive Advertising Bureau have developed guidelines for the usage of data in advertising, delineating best practices and principles. Principles such as legitimate consent, anonymization, and data minimization must be adhered to when collecting and analyzing user data.

Despite ethical considerations, the potential advantages of employing analytics and data-driven decision making for the monetization of streaming platforms cannot be disregarded. Instead of relying on guesswork or generalized assumptions, data-driven strategies enable platforms to make informed choices. This, in turn, enhances user experiences, optimizes revenue generation, and allows for continuous improvement and adaptation.

Efficient utilization of analytics necessitates investment in the requisite infrastructure and talent by streaming platforms. Data collection encompasses a wide range of sources, including user registrations, cookies, and device-specific information. Additionally, platforms can employ advanced analytics tools to extract insights from the data collected. This may entail segmentation, predictive modeling, or even machine learning algorithms in order to automate decision-making processes.

The analysis of user data becomes particularly important when it comes to advertising on streaming platforms. By comprehending user demographics, preferences, and viewing habits, platforms can deliver targeted ads that are more likely to resonate with their audience. This not only enhances the effectiveness of advertising campaigns but also maximizes revenue potential through heightened click-through rates and conversions.

Furthermore, analytics can be utilized to measure the success of advertising campaigns and track return on investment (ROI). Metrics such as viewability, completion rates, and engagement levels aid advertisers and platform operators in comprehending the impact of their campaigns. This information can then be used to refine targeting strategies and optimize ad placements, leading to improved monetization prospects.

In conclusion, analytics and data-driven decision making are indispensable for the monetization of streaming platforms. By collecting and analyzing user data, platforms can gain insights into user behavior, personalize experiences, and effectively target advertising. However, it is critical to approach data usage ethically, ensuring user privacy and maintaining transparency. When executed ethically and strategically, analytics can serve as a powerful tool for driving revenue generation and enhancing user satisfaction in the ever-evolving landscape of streaming media.

As a social science researcher, social entrepreneur, documentary filmmaker, nonprofit executive, and the Chairman and CEO of a broadcast media streaming network, I have firsthand witnessed the transformative potential of analytics in the media industry. The insights derived from data analysis have not only shaped content strategies and advertising campaigns but have also been instrumental in creating personalized experiences for users. It is my belief that in the era of streaming media, wherein user preferences and engagement are the key drivers of success, analytics and data-driven decision making will continue to play a pivotal role in monetization strategies. The ethical and responsible utilization of data will be paramount in maintaining user trust and furthering the growth of streaming platforms.

6

Chapter 6: Operational Considerations for Streaming Platforms

Content Management and Metadata

Content management serves as the essential foundation for any successful streaming platform. It encompasses the necessary processes and systems that facilitate the organization, storage, and retrieval of digital content. The absence of proper content management can rapidly result in a chaotic maze of audio and video files on a streaming platform. Inadequate content management not only impedes users from finding the desired content but also detrimentally impacts the overall user experience.

To surmount these challenges, content tagging assumes a vital role in content management. By assigning descriptive tags to the content, it becomes easier for users to search for and discover specific audio and video streams. These tags can be based on various characteristics such as genre, artist, topic, mood, or language. Employing tags provides users with a quick overview and context of the content, thereby augmenting its discoverability and increasing user engagement.

However, effective content tagging alone does not ensure optimal stream organization. Streaming platforms must also employ sophisticated search algorithms to process user queries and deliver relevant results. These algorithms aim to comprehend the intended meaning behind a user's search, subsequently presenting the most appropriate and accurate results. These algorithms take into consideration factors like relevance, popularity, and user behavior to determine the ranking of search results.

Metadata plays a critical role in attaining seamless and efficient content management. Metadata refers to additional information about the audio or video stream that surpasses basic file data. It comprises an elaborate description of the content, including its title, description, duration, release date, and other pertinent details. Metadata amplifies the searchability and discoverability of content by enabling search engines and algorithms to accurately understand and interpret the stream.

Metadata is structured using standardized formats and schemas. One such widely-used schema in the streaming industry is the Dublin Core Metadata Initiative (DCMI). DCMI provides a framework for describing different attributes of digital resources, including audio and video streams. Its standardized format guarantees interoperability and facilitates resource discovery across various platforms and systems.

Within the DCMI schema, diverse metadata elements contribute to a comprehensive description of audio and video streams. The title element serves as the stream's name, often reflecting its content or purpose. The description element provides a more detailed summary of the stream, offering context and additional information. The duration element specifies the stream's length, assisting users in planning their viewing or listening accordingly.

Other crucial metadata elements encompass the creator, contributor, and publisher. The creator identifies the primary individual or entity responsible for producing the stream, while the contributor acknowledges any secondary parties who have made significant contributions. The publisher signifies the entity responsible for making the stream accessible to the public.

In addition to these primary metadata elements, several others enhance stream discoverability. The subject element denotes the primary topic or theme of the stream, allowing users to locate content related to specific areas of interest. The language element indicates the stream's primarily presented language, making it easier for users to filter and find content in their preferred language.

Furthermore, other metadata elements such as audience, coverage, rights, and format further enhance the comprehension and organization of streams. The audience element defines the targeted audience or age group for the stream, enabling content providers to offer personalized recommendations. The coverage element reveals the geographical or temporal context of the stream, aiding users in identifying content relevant to specific regions or periods.

The rights element outlines the copyright status or usage restrictions associated with the stream, ensuring compliance with legal and ethical guidelines. Lastly, the format element describes the stream's technical specifications, such as file type, resolution, and compression method. This information enables streaming platforms to optimize the stream for different devices and adapt to diverse bandwidth capabilities.

By implementing effective content management and leveraging metadata standards like DCMI, streaming platforms can revolutionize the user experience. With organized and easily discoverable content, users can swiftly find and engage with streams that align with their interests. As a social entrepreneur and documentary filmmaker, I acknowledge the profound impact of user engagement and the role that effective content management plays in achieving this goal.

Streaming platforms that prioritize content management and metadata also benefit from improved insights and analytics. The structured metadata allows platforms to analyze user behavior, preferences, and consumption patterns, providing valuable data for content curation and personalized recommendations. This data-driven approach enables platforms to continually optimize their offerings and enhance the overall user experience.

In conclusion, content management and metadata serve as fundamental pillars in organizing and optimizing streaming platforms. By effectively tagging content and utilizing sophisticated search algorithms, seamless stream discoverability is ensured. Metadata, structured using standardized formats like DCMI, furnishes additional contextual information, allowing search engines and algorithms to accurately interpret and present relevant results. By prioritizing content management and leveraging metadata, streaming platforms can establish a user-centric experience that fosters engagement and enables content providers to better understand and cater to their audience's preferences.

Scalability and Infrastructure

Scalability is a crucial factor to consider in the realm of streaming media. As someone well-versed in social entrepreneurship and holding the esteemed positions of Chairman and CEO of a broadcast media streaming network, I have personally witnessed the daunting obstacles that arise when a streaming platform fails to accommodate a growing audience. In this particular subchapter, we will delve into the nuances of scalability and the infrastructure requirements imperative for supporting a thriving streaming platform.

In the context of streaming media, scalability refers to the capacity to handle an increasing number of users and the resulting data traffic without compromising the stream's quality. Achieving seamless scalability hinges upon considering several factors such as server capacity, Content Delivery Network (CDN) integration, and load balancing.

Server capacity is a foundational aspect of any streaming platform. It primarily involves storing and delivering media content to end-users. As the user base expands, the demand for server capacity also significantly increases. It is crucial to implement a scalable server infrastructure capable of handling a surge in users and timely content delivery. Failure to cater to this demand can lead to buffering issues, content delivery delays, and ultimately, a poor user experience.

One viable strategy to ensure server scalability is leveraging cloud-based server infrastructure. Esteemed cloud platforms such as Amazon

Web Services (AWS) and Microsoft Azure offer elastic computing resources that easily scale up or down based on demand. This adaptability allows streaming platforms to allocate additional server resources during periods of increased user volume and downsize during periods of lower demand. By taking advantage of cloud-based server infrastructure, streaming platforms can bypass the inconveniences and expenses associated with maintaining physical servers. Additionally, they can guarantee a seamless streaming experience for their users.

Another essential aspect of scalability is incorporating a Content Delivery Network (CDN). A CDN encompasses a geographically distributed network of strategically placed servers across the globe. The distribution of media content across multiple servers allows CDNs to minimize latency and expedite content delivery to users, regardless of their geographical location. CDNs cache content within various edge servers to eliminate the need for all clients to connect to the main server. Consequently, as the user base expands, CDNs can meet heightened demand by serving content from the closest edge server, thereby reducing latency and enhancing performance.

Incorporating a CDN into a streaming platform entails several steps. First, the media content must be replicated and distributed among the CDN servers, a process known as content synchronization. The streaming platform must guarantee that content remains synchronized across all CDN servers to ensure users consistently receive up-to-date and consistent material. Moreover, the streaming platform must configure DNS records to direct users to the appropriate CDN servers based on their location. This ensures that users are automatically routed to the nearest server, thereby minimizing latency and optimizing content delivery.

Load balancing stands as another vital aspect of scalability. Load balancing involves equitably distributing incoming data traffic across multiple servers to prevent any one server from becoming overwhelmed by demand. By evenly sharing the workload, streaming platforms can ensure that each server operates within its capacity, thus maintaining optimal performance and eliminating bottlenecks.

There are several strategies for implementing load balancing within a streaming platform. One method involves utilizing a load balancer that distributes incoming data traffic among multiple servers based on predetermined rules. These rules are established based on factors such as server capacity, current load, or geographical location. Load balancers continuously monitor the health of each server and redirect traffic away from servers experiencing issues, ensuring a seamless and uninterrupted streaming experience for users.

Another load balancing strategy involves implementing session persistence. Session persistence ensures that a user remains connected to the same server throughout their streaming session. This proves particularly essential for platforms requiring user authentication or maintaining stateful connections. By preserving session persistence, streaming platforms can deliver a consistent user experience and minimize the need for frequent session reestablishment.

Effectively implementing load balancing necessitates continuous monitoring of server and network performance. Monitoring tools and performance metrics aid in identifying potential bottlenecks or issues, enabling streaming platforms to proactively address them. Additionally, load testing can simulate scenarios involving high user traffic, allowing platforms to evaluate their scalability and identify any weaknesses or limitations.

To conclude, scalability represents a pivotal aspect of streaming media platforms. By considering factors such as server capacity, CDN integration, and load balancing, streaming platforms can ensure seamless scalability and deliver a high-quality streaming experience to their users. Leveraging cloud-based server infrastructure, incorporating a CDN, and implementing effective load balancing strategies stand as crucial steps towards achieving this desired scalability. Witnessing first-hand the transformative power of scalable infrastructure in my capacity as Chairman and CEO of a broadcast media streaming network, I am confident that by implementing the strategies outlined in this sub-chapter, streaming platforms can successfully navigate the challenges of scalability and establish themselves as leaders in the ever-evolving world of streaming media.

Security and Content Protection

Encryption serves as a crucial pillar of security in streaming media. By employing encryption techniques to audio and video data, one can effectively safeguard it from unauthorized access and manipulation during transmission. Put simply, encryption involves converting data into complex codes that can only be deciphered by individuals possessing the appropriate decryption keys. Advanced encryption algorithms, such as the Advanced Encryption Standard (AES), are utilized to ensure the confidentiality and integrity of the streaming content. Through the implementation of AES encryption, each packet of data is protected with a unique key, rendering it nearly impossible for malicious actors to intercept, decipher, or alter the transmitted content.

Digital watermarking is another significant technique utilized to safeguard streaming media against unauthorized use and piracy. This process entails embedding undetectable identification information within the audio or video content in a manner that resists easy removal or tampering. These watermarks operate as a digital fingerprint, enabling content owners to track and establish ownership in case of unauthorized distribution or copyright infringement. Additionally, digital watermarks can contain additional metadata, facilitating the identification of authorized users and the management of their access to specific content. By implementing robust digital watermarking mechanisms, streaming platforms can ensure the protection, traceability, and control of their content.

User authentication represents another vital aspect of security and content protection within streaming media. By verifying the identities of individuals accessing their content and establishing their levels of authorization, streaming platforms can ensure the authenticity of users. User authentication mechanisms can take various forms, including username and password combinations, two-factor authentication, or biometric identification. These measures not only protect against unauthorized access but also enable content providers to deliver personalized experiences, customized recommendations, and user-specific settings. In addition to safeguarding the platform and its content, robust user authentication enhances user trust and confidence in the streaming service.

Mitigating piracy and preventing unauthorized access poses a significant challenge in the realm of streaming media. As technology advances, pirates continuously develop new methods to circumvent security protocols and illegally distribute copyrighted content. However, there are several strategies that can be employed to mitigate these risks. For example, digital rights management (DRM) technologies can be utilized to enforce licensing agreements and restrict unauthorized copying or redistribution of content. DRM systems leverage encryption and authentication techniques to control access to digital media and hinder unauthorized copying or sharing. Furthermore, they enable content providers to define and enforce usage policies, such as time-limited access, device restrictions, or limited viewing quality. DRM technologies have proven to be effective deterrents against piracy and have played a crucial role in safeguarding the interests of content creators and distributors.

Apart from DRM technologies, watermarking techniques can also play a pivotal role in piracy prevention. By embedding unique watermarks tailored to each authorized user, traceability can be established, making it easier to identify any unauthorized sharing or distribution of content and trace it back to the source. This not only acts as a deterrent to potential pirates but also establishes legal accountability in the event of copyright infringement.

It is important to recognize that the security and content protection landscape within streaming media is constantly evolving. New vulnerabilities and threats emerge regularly, necessitating the implementation of dynamic and adaptive security measures. Collaboration between content providers, technology companies, and regulatory bodies is essential in remaining ahead of the curve and ensuring the continuous protection of streaming media.

In conclusion, security concerns and content protection are pivotal aspects in the world of streaming media. Encryption, digital watermarking, user authentication, and piracy prevention techniques all play vital roles in safeguarding the confidentiality, integrity, and traceability of audio and video content. By implementing robust security measures and remaining vigilant in the face of emerging threats, streaming platforms can maintain the trust and confidence of their users while protecting the interests of content creators and distributors. As the Chairman and CEO of a broadcast media streaming network, I acknowledge the significance of these measures and am devoted to ensuring the highest levels of security and content protection within our platform.

Customer Support and Engagement

Customer Support and Engagement play a pivotal role in the success of any streaming media platform. In the current landscape of intense competition, where users have a multitude of options at their disposal, it is imperative to deliver exceptional customer service in order to attract and retain a loyal user base. This subchapter underscores the significance of customer support and engagement in maintaining a devoted user base. It offers strategies for effective customer support, feedback management, and community building.

1. Understanding the Significance of Customer Support:
    a. Before delving into strategies for effective customer support, it is essential to comprehend its criticality. Customer support not only aids users in navigating the platform and resolving technical issues but also builds trust and loyalty. When users encounter problems or inquiries, proactive and dependable customer support can significantly impact

their overall experience. By offering top-notch customer service, a streaming media platform not only fosters customer loyalty but also earns a reputation for being reliable and user-friendly.

2. Strategies for Effective Customer Support:

a. Prompt and Responsive Communication: The initial step towards providing exceptional customer support involves ensuring prompt and responsive communication. Users should have easy access to the support team through various channels such as email, phone, live chat, or even social media platforms. Furthermore, it is crucial to respond to user queries and issues in a timely manner, ideally within 24 hours. This demonstrates to users that their concerns hold value and helps build trust and satisfaction.

b. Knowledgeable Support Staff: The customer support staff must possess a deep knowledge of the platform and its features, as well as a thorough understanding of common user issues and their resolutions. Regular training sessions and workshops can help keep the support team updated and equipped to handle any user query or technical issue that may arise.

c. Personalized Assistance: Providing personalized assistance can greatly enhance the user experience. By taking the time to understand each user's specific needs and offering tailored solutions, the support team can make users feel valued and appreciated. This can be accomplished through features like screen sharing, interactive tutorials, or personalized troubleshooting guides.

d. Self-Service Options: In addition to personalized assistance, self-service options can empower users to independently resolve common issues. A comprehensive knowledge base, frequently asked questions (FAQ) section, or video tutorials can provide users with the resources they need to solve minor issues on their own, saving both time and resources for the support team.

3. Feedback Management: Feedback from users is an invaluable tool that can help identify areas for improvement, uncover bugs, and gain insights into users' preferences and needs. Effective feedback management involves actively seeking feedback, analyzing it, and implementing necessary changes based on user suggestions. Here are some strategies to consider:

   a. User Surveys: Regularly conducting user surveys can provide valuable insights into user satisfaction levels, identify areas for improvement, and gather suggestions for new features or content. Surveys can be distributed via email, embedded in the platform itself, or conducted through third-party survey tools.

   b. Feedback Channels: Providing multiple channels for users to submit feedback, such as dedicated feedback forms, email addresses, or even direct messaging through social media platforms, helps make the process more accessible and convenient. Users should feel encouraged and supported when sharing their thoughts and opinions.

   c. Analyzing and Acting on Feedback: Collecting feedback is merely the first step; the subsequent crucial step is to analyze the data and take action. This may involve prioritizing user suggestions, addressing bugs or technical issues, or incorporating new features based on user preferences. Transparently communicating these changes to users helps foster a sense of engagement and community.

4. Community Building: Cultivating a sense of community among users can significantly enhance the streaming media experience. When users feel connected and engaged with the platform and its community, they are more likely to remain loyal and actively participate. Here are some strategies for community building:

a. User Forums and Discussion Boards: Establishing a dedicated space for users to interact with each other, ask questions, share recommendations, and discuss relevant topics can help foster a sense of community. Moderators can ensure that discussions remain respectful and productive.

b. Social Media Engagement: Leveraging social media platforms to engage with users, share updates, and initiate conversations can help create a vibrant online community. Responding to user comments and messages promptly adds a personal touch and shows users that their voices are valued.

c. Exclusive Events and Rewards: Hosting exclusive events such as virtual screenings, Q&A sessions with industry experts, or giveaways can help create anticipation and excitement among users. Offering rewards or incentives for active participation, such as badges or exclusive content, further fosters a sense of community.

In conclusion, customer support and engagement are paramount for maintaining a loyal user base in the streaming media industry. By prioritizing prompt and responsive communication, personalized assistance, self-service options, and effective feedback management, streaming platforms can enhance user satisfaction, build trust, and foster a vibrant community. By implementing these strategies, my streaming media network aims to provide an exceptional streaming experience and build lasting relationships with our users.

Performance Monitoring and Analytics

Performance monitoring and analytics offer invaluable insights into various aspects of streaming, including stream quality, user experience, and audience engagement. By closely monitoring these metrics, we can identify areas for improvement and implement data-informed strategies to enhance the overall streaming experience.

To commence, let us discuss the significance of key performance indicators (KPIs) in evaluating the performance of streaming platforms. KPIs are essential metrics that allow us to quantitatively assess the effectiveness of our streaming service. They assist us in tracking important aspects such as stream uptime, buffering rate, video start time, and playback quality. By establishing KPIs, we establish a benchmark to measure our performance and identify any discrepancies or areas of concern.

One of the fundamental KPIs for streaming platforms is stream uptime. This metric measures the percentage of time the stream remains available to users without any interruptions or downtime. It is crucial to maintain a high stream uptime to keep users engaged and satisfied with the platform. Any disruption in the stream can lead to frustrations and potentially drive users away. By continuously monitoring stream uptime, we can promptly address any technical issues and ensure a reliable streaming service.

Another vital KPI is buffering rate. Buffering occurs when the stream pauses to load more content, causing a delay in playback. High buffering rates can significantly impact the user experience and result in user dissatisfaction. By monitoring buffering rates, we can identify bottlenecks in the streaming infrastructure and take appropriate measures to optimize content delivery.

Video start time is another key KPI to consider. This metric measures the time it takes for a video to begin playing after a user initiates playback. Lengthy video start times can lead to user frustration, prompting them to abandon the stream altogether. By constantly monitoring and minimizing video start times, we can ensure a seamless and enjoyable streaming experience for our users.

Beyond these specific KPIs, various data visualization techniques can greatly enhance our understanding and analysis of streaming performance. Visualizing data through charts, graphs, and dashboards enables us to gain insights quickly and make informed decisions. Data visualization helps us identify trends, patterns, and outliers, enabling us to pinpoint areas of improvement more efficiently.

We can utilize data visualization tools to create real-time dashboards that display streaming performance metrics at a glance. These dashboards can be customized to display key metrics such as stream uptime, buffering rate, video start time, and playback quality. By having these metrics readily available, we can identify any discrepancies or issues as they occur and take immediate action to resolve them.

Another valuable aspect of performance monitoring and analytics is the ability to track audience engagement. Alongside technical metrics, tracking engagement metrics such as viewer retention, average watch time, and drop-off points can provide valuable insights into user behavior and preferences. By understanding how users interact with our content, we can curate and optimize our streaming platform to better cater to their needs.

Continuous improvement strategies are essential in the world of streaming media. Technology and user preferences are constantly evolving, and it is crucial to stay ahead of the curve. By leveraging performance monitoring and analytics, we can identify opportunities for improvement and implement changes to enhance the streaming experience continuously.

A key strategy for continuous improvement is A/B testing. Through A/B testing, we can experiment with different variables, such as stream quality, video encoding settings, or user interface designs, and measure the impact on user experience. By testing variations, we can identify the most effective options and make data-informed decisions to enhance our streaming platform.

In conclusion, performance monitoring and analytics play a pivotal role in optimizing streaming platforms. By establishing key performance indicators, visualizing data, and implementing continuous improvement strategies, we can ensure a seamless, engaging, and user-centric streaming experience. As an individual with experience as a social science researcher, social entrepreneur, documentary filmmaker, nonprofit executive, and streaming network CEO, I have witnessed the transformative power of data-driven insights in the world of streaming media. With the right tools and analytics in place, we can continue to push the boundaries of audio and video streaming and deliver exceptional content to audiences worldwide.

Chapter 7: Streaming Production Personnel

Audio Production Personnel

Before delving into the specific roles, it is imperative to acknowledge the interdisciplinary nature of audio production. This process encompasses a collective of professionals from diverse fields who converge to create a seamless audio experience. From engineers to sound designers, each member of the audio production personnel contributes their distinct expertise to the collective objective of delivering captivating audio content.

One of the most prominent roles in audio production is that of the audio engineer. These skilled practitioners are entrusted with the responsibility of recording, editing, and mixing audio. They work in close collaboration with artists, producers, and other team members to capture the desired sound, ensuring its freedom from any technical glitches or inconsistencies. Audio engineers possess profound knowledge of recording techniques, signal processing, and audio equipment, which enables them to optimize the recorded material.

Another pivotal role within the audio production team is that of the sound designer. Distinct from the audio engineer, who primarily concentrates on the capturing and manipulation of audio during the recording process, sound designers are involved in post-production.

Using their creative instincts, they enhance the audio quality by incorporating special effects, constructing an immersive soundscape, and ensuring synchronization between audio and visual elements. Sound designers also wield a crucial influence on storytelling by using sound to elicit emotions, instill tension, and elevate the overall narrative of a media production.

One might question how to guarantee the audio reaches the listeners in the best possible quality. To address this, we turn to the role of the broadcast engineer. These professionals specialize in broadcasting systems and transmission, ensuring a seamless delivery of the audio signal across various platforms. Broadcast engineers operate cutting-edge technology to both maintain and optimize audio equipment, ensuring its compliance with industry standards. Additionally, they collaborate with network administrators to guarantee the delivery of high-quality audio content to viewers worldwide via streaming platforms.

Another important role within the audio production personnel is that of the ADR (Automated Dialogue Replacement) mixer. ADR mixers are responsible for integrating dialogue seamlessly into post-production. This technique is commonly employed in film and television to replace or enhance dialogue recorded during the production phase with audio of higher quality. ADR mixers possess expertise in synchronizing dialogue while matching the acoustic qualities of the original recording location, thereby providing a seamless listening experience for the audience.

In addition to these core roles, numerous other positions within audio production significantly contribute to the overall success of a project. These encompass Foley artists, music producers, voice-over artists, and audio post-production executives, among others. Each role entails specific responsibilities, all of which converge towards the common objective of creating exceptional audio content.

For instance, Foley artists are experts in recreating sound effects using various props and materials. They play a vital role in instilling depth and texture to the audio, thereby immersing the audience fully in the sonic world created for a production. Foley artists are renowned for their creativity and meticulous attention to detail, meticulously reproducing sounds that might be overlooked during the natural recording process.

On the other hand, music producers collaborate closely with artists to breathe life into their musical vision. They oversee the entirety of the recording process, ensuring that the music production adheres to the highest standards. Music producers possess expertise in both the technical and artistic aspects of audio production, working jointly with musicians, sound engineers, and other professionals to achieve a cohesive and engrossing sound.

Voice-over artists represent another essential component of the audio production personnel. They lend their voices to various media productions, including commercials, documentaries, and animated films. Voice-over artists exhibit stellar vocal abilities, as well as the capability to bring characters and narratives to life through their delivery. They work closely with directors and producers to effectively convey the desired tone and emotion through their voice.

Lastly, audio post-production executives assume a crucial role in overseeing the entire audio production process. They are entrusted with the responsibility of managing budgets, schedules, and resources, ensuring the project remains on track. Audio post-production executives work closely with all members of the audio production personnel to ensure that the final product meets the highest quality standards and is delivered punctually.

In conclusion, the world of audio production proves to be a captivating and multifaceted domain, populated by skilled professionals who bring forth their unique skills and expertise to create captivating audio content. From audio engineers to sound designers, each member of the audio production personnel assumes a vital role in fostering the highest quality audio experience for the audience. As we continue to explore the foundations of broadcast media streaming, it remains crucial to acknowledge and appreciate the immense contributions of these individuals who diligently operate behind the scenes, thereby bringing the enchantment of sound to our screens.

Video Production Personnel

In the realm of video production, there are several fundamental positions that must be filled to ensure a smooth and efficient operation. Each member of the team brings a distinct set of skills and expertise which harmoniously combine to create a seamless final product. Allow me to provide an overview of the various roles and their respective responsibilities.

The director assumes the role of the leading figure, overseeing all aspects of the production process. Possessing a discerning eye for detail and a strong creative vision, the director guides the team in shaping the narrative and visual style of the content. They work closely with the producers and scriptwriters, translating the written word into visually captivating elements that resonate with the intended target audience. As the Chief Executive Officer of our network, I adopt a hands-on approach to directing, drawing upon my experience as a documentary filmmaker to ensure that our content maintains the utmost standards of quality.

Next in line are the producers, who play a pivotal role in coordinating every facet of the production. They are responsible for proficiently managing budgets, securing necessary resources, and ensuring that deadlines are met. Producers also oversee casting decisions, working closely with the director to select the ideal talent to bring the script to life. Their exceptional organizational skills are crucial in keeping the production on track and within budget. As a social entrepreneur and nonprofit executive, I comprehend the significance of budgeting and resource management, and my experience guides our production team in this aspect.

Scriptwriters, also acknowledged as screenwriters, are the masterminds behind the storylines and dialogue which breathe life into our productions. These highly skilled individuals collaborate closely with the director to craft compelling narratives that resonate with our target audience. Striking a delicate balance between dialogue, action, and emotion, scriptwriters mold the scripts in a way that engages and captivates viewers. Their creativity is paramount in constructing stories that leave a lasting impression on the minds and hearts of audiences long after they have consumed our content. As a social science researcher, I possess a profound understanding of the psychology behind storytelling and leverage this knowledge to provide valuable insights to our scriptwriters.

The cinematographer, also referred to as the director of photography, assumes responsibility for the visual elements of the production. Using their artistic eye and technical expertise, they bring the director's vision to life through the camera lens. In close collaboration with the lighting and camera crew, the cinematographer captures perfect shots, establishing the desired mood and atmosphere. A profound understanding of composition, lighting, and framing techniques is essential for the cinematographer in order to effectively communicate the intended emotions to the audience. As a documentary filmmaker, I appreciate the significance of visual storytelling and work closely with our cinematographers to achieve the desired visual aesthetic for our productions.

The editing team plays a crucial role in the post-production process. They take all the footage captured during the shoot and transform it into a cohesive and visually appealing final product. Skillful editing has the capacity to enhance storytelling by seamlessly weaving together different scenes, adjusting the pace, and creating seamless transitions. The editors work closely with the director to ensure that the final product aligns with the creative vision. In addition, they employ special effects, graphics, and sound design to heighten the overall impact of the production. As the CEO of our network, I recognize the power of post-production and its influence on the final product. I collaborate closely with our editing team, providing guidance on the narrative structure and ensuring that the viewer's experience is seamless and engaging.

Lastly, the audio engineers are responsible for capturing and enhancing the sound elements of the production. Their expertise lies in recording high-quality audio and creating immersive soundscapes that enhance the storytelling process. From capturing dialogue to designing ambient sound effects, audio engineers play a critical role in creating an immersive audio experience for the audience. As an experienced documentary filmmaker, I understand the importance of quality audio in capturing the essence and emotions of a scene. I work closely with our audio engineers to meticulously craft each sound element to enhance the viewer's experience.

In conclusion, the success of a broadcast media streaming network depends on a skilled and diverse team of video production personnel. Each member of the team brings their unique skills and expertise, collaborating closely to bring the director's vision to life. From the director and producer to the scriptwriters, cinematographers, editors, and audio engineers, each role is indispensable in creating captivating content that resonates with audiences worldwide. As the Chairman and CEO of our network, I take pride in leading this team of talented individuals, relying on my experiences as a social science researcher, social entrepreneur, documentary filmmaker, and nonprofit executive to drive our network's success. Together, we are committed to delivering the highest quality productions that entertain, educate, and inspire viewers worldwide.

Executive and Administrative Personnel

To commence, let us delve into the fundamental definition and context of executive and administrative personnel in a formal setting. Within the realm of a streaming network, executive personnel pertains to top-level decision-makers who hold the responsibility of overseeing the overall direction and triumph of the organization. These individuals possess extensive industry experience and knowledge, as well as the ability to think strategically and navigate the constantly evolving media landscape.

On the other hand, administrative personnel fulfill a critical supportive role in the day-to-day operations of the network. They are accountable for managing administrative tasks, coordinating schedules, and ensuring the seamless functioning of various departments within the organization. The presence of both executive and administrative personnel is indispensable in maintaining an efficient workflow, managing resources, and accomplishing the network's goals and objectives.

The responsibilities of executive personnel within a broadcast media streaming network are multifaceted and demanding. As the Chief Executive Officer (CEO) of my own network, I am accountable for formulating strategic goals and objectives, devising long-term plans, and overseeing the overall trajectory of the organization. This encompasses making crucial decisions regarding content acquisition, distribution strategies, and technological advancements to ensure that the network remains at the forefront of the industry.

Furthermore, executive personnel bear the responsibility of establishing and nurturing relationships with key stakeholders, such as content creators, advertisers, and investors. These relationships are vital for securing partnerships, funding, and ensuring the network's sustained growth and success. Additionally, it is the duty of executive personnel to lead and inspire the entire organization, fostering a culture of innovation, collaboration, and excellence.

In order to effectively fulfill these responsibilities, executive personnel must possess a distinct set of skills and qualifications. A comprehensive understanding of the broadcast media streaming industry is of paramount importance, as well as a keen awareness of emerging trends and technologies. The ability to analyze data, evaluate market conditions, and anticipate consumer behavior is crucial for making well-informed decisions that will drive the network's success.

Moreover, executive personnel must possess superior communication skills, capable of articulating the network's vision and goals to both internal and external stakeholders. Leadership skills, including the ability to inspire, motivate, and empower a diverse team, are key to fostering a positive work environment and cultivating a shared sense of purpose and dedication. Furthermore, a robust business acumen, financial literacy, and strategic thinking are indispensable in navigating the intricate landscape of the media industry.

While executive personnel oversee the bigger picture and set the strategic direction of the network, administrative personnel play an equally indispensable role in ensuring the efficient and smooth operation of day-to-day activities. These individuals bear the responsibility of managing administrative tasks, coordinating schedules, and overseeing the implementation of policies and procedures. Their attention to detail, organizational skills, and ability to perform effectively in fast-paced environments are vital to upholding the network's productivity and efficacy.

Administrative personnel are also accountable for managing budgets, tracking expenses, and providing support to various departments within the organization. This includes coordinating logistics for production teams, managing resources, and ensuring the timely delivery of content to viewers. Their role often necessitates multitasking, problem-solving, and adapting swiftly to changing circumstances.

Furthermore, administrative personnel function as the primary point of contact for internal and external stakeholders, encompassing employees, clients, and vendors. They handle inquiries, resolve conflicts, and furnish the necessary support and resources to ensure a seamless workflow. Excellent communication, organizational, and interpersonal skills are imperative in maintaining effective relationships and fostering a positive working environment.

In conclusion, the role of executive and administrative personnel holds paramount importance in the broadcast media streaming industry. Executive personnel, with their strategic thinking, industry knowledge, and leadership skills, steer the overall direction and success of the organization. Conversely, administrative personnel, with their organizational abilities, attention to detail, and effective communication, ensure the smooth and efficient operation of daily activities. Coalescing harmoniously, these individuals form the core of any streaming network, working together to deliver captivating content to viewers and establish long-term success in the fiercely competitive landscape of the media industry. As the Chairman and CEO of my own broadcast media streaming network, I deeply appreciate the pivotal contributions of both executive and administrative personnel and remain steadfast in my commitment to fostering a dynamic and supportive environment where everyone can thrive and contribute to our shared vision of revolutionizing the world of media streaming.

8

Chapter 8: Live Streaming Events

Equipment and Setup

Cameras:

Capturing high-quality video footage is a critical aspect of live streaming. Therefore, it is essential to invest in good cameras. There are several options available in the market, ranging from professional-grade cameras to consumer-level ones. The choice of camera will depend on factors such as budget, the nature of the event, and the desired level of production quality.

For smaller events or tight budgets, consumer-level cameras or smartphones equipped with high-resolution cameras can be sufficient. Nowadays, smartphones come with impressive video capabilities, allowing users to capture high-definition footage easily. Additionally, many smartphones can seamlessly connect to streaming software or platforms, optimizing workflow efficiency.

On the other hand, larger events or those that require professional-grade video quality necessitate investment in dedicated video cameras. These cameras offer advanced features like interchangeable lenses, manual controls, and higher bitrates, delivering more control and depth in video production. Popular choices include DSLR cameras or camcorders, which offer various options for video resolutions and frame rates.

Furthermore, it is crucial to consider the number of cameras needed for the live stream. For multi-camera setups, additional cameras, tripods, or camera mounts are required to ensure stable footage. The number of cameras and their placement will depend on the event's nature and the desired angles to capture.

Audio Systems:

While video quality is important, audio quality plays an equally significant role in providing a captivating live streaming experience. Poor audio can greatly diminish the impact of content and leave viewers feeling disconnected. Consequently, investing in a high-quality audio system is vital.

At a minimum, a basic audio setup should include a microphone and a sound mixer. There are various types of microphones available, such as dynamic microphones, condenser microphones, and lavalier microphones. The choice of microphone will depend on factors like the event venue, ambient noise levels, and the proximity of the microphone to the speaker or performers.

Dynamic microphones are durable and can handle high sound pressure levels, making them suitable for capturing live performances or events with loud backgrounds. On the other hand, condenser microphones offer more detailed and accurate sound reproduction, making them ideal for capturing delicate sounds or vocals.

In addition to the microphone, a sound mixer is essential for adjusting audio levels, adding effects, and controlling the overall sound output. A sound mixer enables users to balance audio from different sources, such as microphones, instruments, or playback devices.

Encoding Devices:

Once high-quality video and audio have been captured, the next step is encoding or compressing the data for streaming over the internet. Encoding devices convert raw video and audio files into a format that is compatible with various streaming platforms and easily transmitted over the internet.

There are different types of encoding devices available, ranging from hardware encoders to software-based solutions. Hardware encoders are standalone devices that directly connect to cameras or audio systems, offering real-time encoding capabilities and streamlining the workflow. These devices often include built-in features such as network connectivity, recording capabilities, and integrated streaming platform compatibility.

Software-based encoding solutions, on the other hand, are computer programs or applications that utilize the processing power of a computer to encode video and audio. These solutions provide more flexibility and customization options, allowing users to fine-tune encoding settings based on streaming requirements.

Internet Connectivity:

Having a reliable and high-speed internet connection is crucial for successful live streaming. Insufficient bandwidth or unstable internet connectivity can lead to buffering issues, stream interruptions, and a poor viewing experience for the audience.

Before a live streaming event, it is essential to assess the internet connectivity at the venue. Online speed testing tools can be used to check the upload speed of the internet connection. It is important to ensure that the upload speed is sufficient to handle the bitrate of the live stream. As a general guideline, a stable upload speed that is at least double the bitrate of the stream is recommended for a smooth live streaming experience.

If the venue's internet connection is not strong enough, alternative options such as using a dedicated cellular network or satellite internet connection should be considered. Many encoding devices or software solutions offer the flexibility to use multiple internet connections simultaneously, providing added redundancy and stability.

Testing and Troubleshooting:

Thoroughly testing and troubleshooting the equipment and setup is vital before going live with a stream. This includes testing cameras, audio systems, encoding devices, and internet connectivity to ensure everything is in working order.

Cameras can be tested by setting up practice shots or recording a short video to check for any issues with video quality, focus, or stability. Conducting sound checks using various microphones or audio sources helps in checking the audio system to ensure that sound levels are balanced and clear.

Next, encoding devices or software solutions should be tested by setting up a test stream and monitoring stream quality, frame rates, and encoding settings. Any necessary adjustments should be made to optimize video and audio quality and minimize potential latency or buffering issues.

Finally, a live stream test using the actual internet connection that will be used for the event should be conducted. This test helps identify any potential bandwidth or connectivity issues and allows for optimizing stream settings accordingly.

Conclusion:

Setting up equipment and ensuring a seamless live streaming experience requires careful planning, investment, and testing. By investing in good cameras, audio systems, encoding devices, and having a reliable internet connection, professional-quality live streams can be created that engage and captivate the audience. Thoroughly testing and troubleshooting the setup before going live is crucial to addressing any issues. With the right equipment and a solid setup, the full potential of live streaming can be unlocked, delivering high-quality audio and video experiences to viewers.

Audience Engagement

Incorporating Interactive Features:

A highly effective approach to engaging with one's audience during live streaming events involves the integration of interactive features. These features serve to actively involve viewers and generate a sense of inclusivity. An example of a popular interactive feature is the live chat, which facilitates real-time conversations between viewers and the host. This live chat feature provides an avenue for viewers to pose questions, make comments, and share their thoughts, thereby fostering a sense of community among the audience. Another interactive feature that can be employed is polls. These allow the host to promptly gather viewer feedback and insights. This not only engages viewers but also equips hosts with valuable information to tailor content in a more audience-specific manner to cater to their preferences and interests. Furthermore, incorporating Q&A sessions into the live streaming event promotes a deeper level of engagement. By encouraging viewers to submit questions, the host is able to address specific topics or concerns, resulting in a more personalized experience. It is of utmost importance to allocate sufficient time for these Q&A sessions, as it exemplifies the host's willingness to listen to and engage with the audience's needs.

Integration of Social Media:

In today's era of digital connectivity, incorporating social media platforms into live streaming events plays a pivotal role in enhancing audience engagement. By encouraging viewers to share the live stream on their social media accounts, the event can rapidly attain a broader audience, thereby expanding the potential for engagement. Additionally, integrating social media within the live stream itself, such as by displaying live tweets or Instagram posts related to the event, further engages viewers. This interactive element allows the audience to actively contribute to ongoing discussions and provides opportunities for the host to acknowledge and respond to their comments or questions in real time.

Utilizing Real-Time Analytics:

For a comprehensive understanding of the impact and effectiveness of content, analyzing audience engagement during live streaming events is crucial. Real-time analytics provide valuable insights into audience behavior, empowering hosts to make informed decisions and adjustments to optimize engagement levels. Through the monitoring of metrics such as viewer count, watch time, and viewer retention, hosts gain a clearer understanding of audience engagement levels. For instance, if viewership declines during a certain segment, the host can adapt the content or delivery to recapture audience interest. Furthermore, analyzing audience interaction with interactive features such as live chat and polls yields valuable feedback on the efficacy and impact of these engagement tactics. This data can then be harnessed to refine and maximize audience engagement in future live streaming events.

Creating an Unforgettable Viewer Experience:

Beyond interactive features and analytics, the creation of a memorable viewer experience is paramount in maximizing audience engagement. The overall production quality, including video and audio clarity, lighting, and set design, significantly influences audience perception of the event. Investing in professional equipment and technical expertise can make a noticeable difference in viewer engagement and enjoyment. In addition, the host's ability to forge a personal connection with the audience is essential. It is imperative that hosts project authenticity and enthusiasm to establish an authentic rapport with viewers. Engaging with the audience entails acknowledging their presence and contributions while promptly responding to their comments and queries, all of which contribute to a positive viewer experience. Moreover, the inclusion of storytelling techniques within the live streaming event can be highly impactful. Engaging narratives and storytelling elements capture the audience's attention, intensifying their engagement. The strategic utilization of emotions, suspense, and surprise sustains viewer interest throughout the event. Lastly, actively involving the audience in decision-making processes, such as allowing them to choose future live streaming event topics or vote on specific aspects of the event, fosters a sense of ownership and investment. By treating the audience as active participants rather than passive spectators, their engagement and loyalty to the event are significantly enhanced.

Conclusion:

This subchapter has explored various strategies for maximizing audience engagement during live streaming events. By incorporating interactive features such as live chat, polls, and Q&A sessions, integrating social media platforms, utilizing real-time analytics, and prioritizing the creation of a memorable viewer experience, hosts can create a more engaging and inclusive environment for their audience. These strategies not only enhance the viewer experience but also provide valuable data to measure audience engagement and optimize future live streaming events.

Monetization Opportunities

One of the most prevalent methods for generating income from live streaming events is through the utilization of ticketed live streams. This particular approach involves charging viewers for access to the live stream, thereby creating a perception of exclusivity and value. Artists, musicians, and performers, amongst others, have successfully employed this model to generate revenue while simultaneously engaging with their audience within a virtual context. By establishing a reasonably priced ticket and providing unique and captivating content, live streamers have the ability to attract a loyal following and produce significant financial gains.

Another variation of the ticketed live stream model is known as the pay-per-view model. This particular method enables viewers to make individual payments for specific events or content within a larger live streaming platform. Pay-per-view models are frequently used for special live events, sports competitions, or eagerly awaited performances. By charging a fee for access to these exclusive experiences, live streamers are able to capitalize on the demand for unique content, therefore delivering a high-quality viewing experience.

In addition to ticketed streams and pay-per-view models, sponsorship deals present an additional avenue for lucrative monetization. Numerous brands and companies are keen to associate themselves with popular live streamers or events, and are therefore willing to pay for sponsorships or advertisement placements. By strategically partnering with likeminded brands, streamers can not only generate revenue but also enhance their credibility and expand their reach to a wider audience. Striking the right balance between promoting sponsored content and preserving the integrity of the live stream is crucial in ensuring a positive viewing experience for the audience.

Merchandise sales represent yet another opportunity for monetization. Similar to traditional concerts or events, live streamers can create and sell branded merchandise to their audience. This can include t-shirts, posters, accessories, or even digital goods such as emojis or virtual items. By offering exclusive merchandise associated with the live stream event, streamers can tap into their fans' desire for memorabilia and generate additional streams of revenue.

Virtual event experiences provide another method for monetizing live streaming. Thanks to advancements in virtual reality and augmented reality technologies, it is now possible to create immersive and interactive experiences for viewers. Streamers can offer virtual meet-and-greets, backstage access, or the opportunity to interact with performers in real-time. By charging a premium for these exceptional experiences, live streamers can enhance the value proposition of their content, attracting viewers who are willing to pay for a more engaging and personalized encounter.

Lastly, the monetization of post-event content should not be disregarded. Even once the live stream event has concluded, the content often retains value. Streamers can repurpose footage into highlights, behind-the-scenes videos, or extended interviews, subsequently offering them for purchase or on a subscription basis. By capitalizing on the demand for on-demand content, streamers can continue generating revenue long after the live stream has finished.

Just like any monetization strategy, it is vital to prioritize the overall user experience. Striking the right balance between revenue generation and the delivery of high-quality and engaging content is crucial in maintaining viewer loyalty and attracting new audiences. Transparent communication, clear pricing structures, and regular feedback from viewers can assist streamers in refining their monetization strategies, ensuring the delivery of value to their audience.

In conclusion, the opportunities for monetizing live streaming events are broad and diverse. Ticketed live streams, pay-per-view models, sponsorship deals, merchandise sales, virtual event experiences, and post-event content monetization all provide unique avenues for generating revenue and engaging with viewers. As a social science researcher, social entrepreneur, documentary filmmaker, nonprofit executive, and the Chairman and CEO of a broadcast media streaming network, I have personally observed the potential of these opportunities. By exploring and implementing these strategies creatively and ethically, live streamers can build sustainable businesses while simultaneously providing exceptional content to their audience.

Chapter 9: Cross-Platform Streaming

Content Adaptation and Optimization

Responsiveness in Design:

The initial step towards content adaptation and optimization entails ensuring compatibility between your content and various screen sizes and resolutions. The key to achieving this lies in employing responsive design techniques. Responsive design refers to the ability of a website or application to automatically adjust its layout and content based on the user's device.

Considering the increasing assortment of devices available in the market, ranging from smartphones to tablets to smart TVs, it is imperative to develop a responsive design that seamlessly adapts to each platform. This requires taking into account factors such as screen size, resolution, and input methods, and tailoring your content accordingly.

Adaptive Bitrate Streaming:

Once you have implemented a responsive design, the subsequent phase involves optimizing the delivery of your media content. Adaptive bitrate streaming is a technique that allows the streaming server to dynamically adjust the quality of the video stream according to the user's network conditions.

By utilizing adaptive bitrate streaming, you can ensure that viewers with slower internet connections can still enjoy your content without encountering buffering or disruptions. This is achieved by encoding the video in multiple quality levels (bitrates) and permitting the streaming server to switch between them based on the user's available bandwidth.

Research has demonstrated that adaptive bitrate streaming can significantly enhance the user experience by reducing buffering time and improving overall video quality. Therefore, it is imperative to integrate this technique within your streaming platform.

Optimization Tailored to Specific Platforms:

In addition to implementing responsive design and adaptive bitrate streaming, it is vital to consider platform-specific optimizations to further enhance the user experience. Each platform possesses its own distinct peculiarities and capabilities, and optimizing your content for each respective platform can greatly impact how it is perceived by your audience.

For instance, mobile platforms typically exhibit limited processing power and battery life; hence, optimizing your content for efficient playback on these devices is crucial. This may entail reducing the video resolution or frame rate, or employing a codec that is more energy efficient.

Conversely, smart TVs and high-end desktop computers are capable of handling higher resolutions and more elaborate content. Therefore, by offering higher-quality videos or interactive features specifically designed for these platforms, you can create a more immersive experience for your audience.

Ultimately, platform-specific optimizations necessitate a comprehensive understanding of the capabilities and limitations of each individual platform. Engaging in research and conducting tests on various platforms can assist in identifying the most effective optimization strategies for each specific platform.

Content Delivery Networks (CDNs):

Content delivery networks (CDNs) play an integral role in ensuring seamless playback across multiple platforms. CDNs consist of a network of servers distributed geographically that cache and distribute your content to viewers based on their location.

By harnessing the geographically dispersed servers of a CDN, you can significantly reduce the distance between your content and your viewers, thereby resulting in faster loading times and smoother playback. CDNs also aid in distributing the load across multiple servers, alleviating strain on your streaming server and ensuring scalability as your audience expands.

When selecting a CDN, it is crucial to consider factors such as the CDN's network coverage, performance capabilities, and pricing. Popular CDNs include Amazon CloudFront, Akamai, and Cloudflare.

In addition to choosing the appropriate CDN, adequately configuring your streaming platform to optimize CDN performance is essential. This might encompass establishing caching rules, enabling compression, and employing efficient protocols such as HTTP/2 or QUIC.

By adhering to these steps, you can adapt and optimize your content for diverse platforms, guaranteeing a seamless and satisfying streaming experience for your audience. It is imperative to stay updated with the latest technologies and best practices in content adaptation and optimization, as the streaming landscape is constantly evolving.

Platform Integration and Distribution

The primary factor to consider when initiating platform integration and distribution is to gain an understanding of the particular requirements of each platform. Every platform, including social media sites, streaming services, and video sharing platforms, has its own set of guidelines and technical specifications when it comes to content integration. To ensure that your content is optimized for each platform, it is vital to familiarize yourself with these requirements.

Once you have obtained a clear understanding of the platform-specific requirements, the subsequent step is to explore application programming interfaces (APIs). These APIs enable you to connect your content to the platform's ecosystem, facilitating seamless integration and distribution. By using APIs, you can transfer data between your streaming media network and the platform, enabling automatic content updates and ensuring that your audience receives the latest offerings.

Partnerships can also play a significant role in platform integration and distribution. Collaborating with relevant organizations, such as content creators, influencers, or industry leaders, can help expand your reach and broaden your audience. Utilizing partnerships allows you to tap into existing networks and benefit from their established user bases. This collaborative approach fosters growth and engagement through cross-promotion of each other's content, creating a mutually beneficial relationship.

Cross-promotion is a key strategy in platform integration and distribution. By promoting your content across various platforms, you can reach a broader audience and take advantage of the unique demographics and user bases associated with each platform. For instance, if your streaming media network primarily focuses on music content, you can utilize social media platforms to promote exclusive interviews and behind-the-scenes footage, encouraging users to engage with your content on your streaming platform.

A productive approach to expand reach and engagement is to leverage user-generated content. Encouraging your audience to create and share their own content related to your streaming media network can significantly enhance your online presence. User-generated content provides fresh and unique perspectives while fostering a sense of community and user engagement. Through the use of hashtags, challenges, and contests, you can actively encourage your audience to participate in creating and sharing content, promoting organic growth and user-driven promotion.

To effectively integrate and distribute content across multiple platforms, it is essential to have a multi-channel distribution strategy. This means strategically selecting and optimizing platforms that align with your target audience and content genre. For example, if your streaming media network focuses on educational content, platforms such as YouTube, Facebook Live, and Vimeo may be suitable choices for reaching a diverse audience. Understanding your audience's preferences, habits, and preferred platforms will enable you to tailor your distribution strategy accordingly.

One aspect that should not be overlooked in platform integration and distribution is the use of analytics. Analytics provide valuable insights into audience behavior, content performance, and engagement metrics. By regularly analyzing your analytics data, you can identify trends, gauge audience preferences, and make data-driven decisions to optimize your platform integration and distribution strategy. These insights will enable you to refine and adapt your content to better resonate with your target audience and enhance engagement.

As technology continues to evolve, it is essential to stay updated with the latest trends and innovations in platform integration and content distribution. Embracing emerging technologies such as virtual reality, augmented reality, and live streaming can provide unique opportunities to engage with your audience in new and exciting ways. By adopting innovation, you can distinguish your streaming media network and position yourself at the forefront of the industry.

In conclusion, platform integration and distribution is a complex process that requires careful consideration and strategic planning. By understanding platform-specific requirements, leveraging APIs and partnerships, implementing cross-promotion and user-generated content strategies, optimizing multi-channel distribution, analyzing analytics, and embracing emerging technologies, you can successfully navigate the landscape of platform integration and distribution. This comprehensive approach will maximize reach, engagement, and growth for your streaming media network, solidifying your position in the ever-evolving world of audio and video streaming.

Analytics and Insights

Analytics and insights serve as indispensable tools for any streaming media platform. By leveraging the data collected during streaming, companies can obtain crucial insights into their audience and their preferences. This data can be utilized to evaluate audience reach, engagement, and retention across various platforms, enabling companies to customize their content and marketing strategies accordingly.

One of the primary metrics in analytics is audience reach. This metric refers to the number of unique viewers or users who have accessed a specific streaming platform or content. By monitoring audience reach, companies can comprehend the popularity and scope of their content. This information is imperative for making well-informed decisions regarding content creation and distribution.

Engagement is another pivotal aspect of analytics and insights. It measures the level of interaction and involvement of viewers with the streamed content. Engagement metrics encompass measurements such as views, likes, shares, comments, and duration of time spent watching a video or listening to audio. Understanding audience engagement aids companies in identifying the content that best resonates with their viewers and optimizing their programming accordingly.

Retention is another significant metric that necessitates consideration. It denotes the streaming platform's ability to retain its audience over time. High retention rates indicate viewer satisfaction with the content and likelihood of continued platform usage. Conversely, low retention rates may suggest a need for content improvements or changes to enhance the user experience. By measuring retention rates, companies can identify areas where improvement is necessary and take appropriate action to keep their audience engaged and loyal.

Cross-platform analytics and insights encompass gauging audience reach, engagement, and retention across diverse platforms. This is particularly relevant in today's digital landscape where viewers consume content on various devices and platforms, including smartphones, tablets, laptops, and smart TVs. By analyzing data from these different platforms, companies can obtain a comprehensive understanding of their audience and their preferences across multiple channels.

Data-driven insights play a crucial role in optimizing content distribution and informing business decisions. By analyzing data collected from various analytics tools and platforms, companies can identify trends, patterns, and audience preferences. These insights can inform content creation, marketing strategies, and even business partnerships. For instance, if data indicates that a specific segment of the audience favors a particular content genre, companies can allocate resources to produce more content in that genre to cater to their audience's preferences.

Data-driven insights can also facilitate well-informed decisions regarding content distribution. For instance, if data indicates that a significant portion of the audience accesses content through mobile devices, companies can prioritize optimizing their mobile app or website to ensure a seamless user experience. Similarly, if data reveals that a particular platform or social media channel generates high levels of engagement, companies can prioritize their marketing efforts on that platform to maximize reach and impact.

Furthermore, data-driven insights can aid companies in identifying emerging opportunities and potential partnerships. By analyzing data on audience demographics, interests, and consumption patterns, companies can identify untapped market segments or potential collaborations with content creators or influencers. These insights provide a competitive advantage by enabling companies to stay ahead of trends and capitalize on new opportunities in the streaming media industry.

It is important to note that analytics and insights are not static but an ongoing process. Companies should continuously collect and analyze data to remain abreast of their audience's preferences, behaviors, and trends. This necessitates investing in robust analytics tools, staying informed about industry best practices, and adapting strategies based on the insights gleaned from the data.

In conclusion, analytics and insights serve as invaluable resources for cross-platform streaming. By evaluating audience reach, engagement, and retention, companies can tailor their content and marketing strategies to maximize impact and profitability. Utilizing data-driven insights enables companies to optimize content distribution, inform business decisions, and identify emerging opportunities in the ever-evolving streaming media landscape. As the streaming media industry continues to expand and evolve, analytics and insights will remain indispensable tools for success in this dynamic and competitive field.

10

Chapter 10: Streaming Media Analytics and Data Insights

Audience Segmentation and Targeting

At the forefront of audience segmentation is the utilization of demographic data. Gaining an understanding of factors such as age, gender, location, education level, and other key demographic information enables streaming platforms to develop targeted content that resonates with specific groups. For instance, by identifying a significant percentage of viewers aged 18-25, a streaming platform may concentrate on providing content that appeals to this young adult demographic, such as music festivals, high-energy sporting events, or cutting-edge fashion shows. Utilizing demographic data also plays a critical role in ensuring that advertising campaigns effectively reach the intended target audience, thus enhancing the efficiency of ad spending.

In addition to demographic data, behavioral data provides valuable insights into viewer preferences and consumption patterns. By monitoring user interactions, browsing history, search queries, and content consumption habits, streaming platforms can acquire a deep understanding of how viewers engage with their services. This data can be used to provide personalized content recommendations, suggesting movies, TV shows, or music based on past viewing habits. For example, if a viewer frequently watches romantic comedies, the streaming platform can recommend similar films within the same genre.

Behavioral data also empowers streaming platforms to optimize their advertising efforts. By analyzing viewer interactions with ads, such as click-through rates and conversions, advertisers can deliver more pertinent and engaging content to their target audience. For instance, if a viewer routinely disregards ads related to home appliances, the streaming platform can tailor and deliver advertisements that align with the viewer's interests, such as travel or lifestyle products.

Psychographic data adds an additional layer of insight into audience segmentation by focusing on viewers' personalities, values, interests, and attitudes. This data is typically obtained through surveys, focus groups, or social media analysis. Psychographic segmentation allows streaming platforms to target individuals based on their unique preferences and motivations. For instance, by identifying a group of viewers who are environmentally conscious and health-oriented, a streaming platform can curate content related to sustainability, organic living, and wellness practices.

By combining demographic, behavioral, and psychographic data, streaming platforms can create highly specific audience segments that, in turn, enhance user experiences. By comprehending the unique characteristics and preferences of different viewer groups, streaming platforms can provide content that caters to their specific needs and interests. This level of personalization not only increases viewer satisfaction, but also encourages prolonged engagement with the platform.

Within the realm of targeted advertising, audience segmentation allows streaming platforms to offer advertisers a more precise and effective means of reaching their desired audience. By categorizing viewers based on their interests, behaviors, and demographics, streaming platforms can provide advertisers with the opportunity to deliver their ads to the most receptive groups. This not only increases the likelihood of viewer engagement, but also maximizes the return on investment for advertisers. For example, if an automotive brand wishes to target viewers interested in luxury cars, the streaming platform can ensure that the brand's ads are shown to viewers in this specific demographic.

While audience segmentation and targeting provide numerous benefits to streaming platforms and advertisers, they also present challenges to navigate. One significant challenge is managing user privacy and data protection. As streaming platforms collect vast amounts of personal data to create audience segments, it is crucial to implement robust security measures and respect user privacy rights. This includes obtaining proper consent, ensuring data encryption, and providing transparent insights into data collection practices.

Another challenge lies in accurately representing the diversity within audience segments. While segmentation allows streaming platforms to cater to specific viewer groups, it is important to avoid perpetuating stereotypes or neglecting the inclusion of underrepresented demographics. Through conducting thorough research and considering a diverse range of demographic factors, streaming platforms can ensure that their content and advertisements resonate with a broad audience.

In conclusion, audience segmentation and targeting constitute an integral aspect of streaming media strategies. By leveraging demographic, behavioral, and psychographic data, streaming platforms can effectively personalize content recommendations and deliver targeted advertising to specific viewer groups. This level of personalization enhances user experiences, increases viewer engagement, and maximizes revenue possibilities for both streaming platforms and advertisers. However, it is essential to navigate the challenges of user privacy and diversity representation in order to fully harness the potential of audience segmentation and targeting in streaming media.

Content Performance Analysis

One of the fundamental methods for evaluating the performance of content is through viewer ratings. These ratings offer valuable insights into the popularity and reception of a specific piece of content.

Historically, ratings have been gathered through surveys or sample audience measurements. However, the rise of streaming platforms has made it more convenient to collect real-time viewer data. This real-time data enables a more precise and timely evaluation of a show's performance.

Another crucial element in content performance analysis is engagement metrics. These metrics gauge the level of audience involvement and interaction with the content. Key engagement metrics encompass average watch time, completion rate, and interactions with interactive elements within the streaming platform. By analyzing these metrics, content creators and streaming platforms can understand how effectively their content captures and retains the attention of viewers.

In addition to viewer ratings and engagement metrics, social media buzz plays a significant role in content performance analysis. Social media platforms have become influential channels for audience engagement, discussion, and promotion. By monitoring mentions, hashtags, and conversations related to a particular show or movie, content creators and streaming platforms can assess the level of interest and excitement generated by their content. Social media buzz offers valuable insights into the reach and impact of a piece of content, informing future content acquisition and production decisions.

Furthermore, content performance analysis is vital in shaping content acquisition strategies. Streaming platforms are constantly searching for engaging and high-performing content to enhance their catalog. By analyzing the performance of different shows and movies, streaming platforms can identify trends, genres, or specific actors that resonate well with their audience. This analysis helps inform decisions about acquiring content that is likely to attract and retain viewers.

Moreover, content performance analysis guides production decisions. By understanding what elements work and what do not, content creators can tailor their storytelling, character development, and production values to better appeal to their target audience. Analysis of viewer ratings, engagement metrics, and social media buzz provides valuable feedback on the success and reception of specific content elements, enabling content creators to refine their approach and deliver content that resonates more effectively.

A comprehensive content performance analysis is also crucial for audience retention strategies. Streaming platforms aim to keep their subscribers engaged and subscribed for the long term. By continuously analyzing the performance of different shows and movies, they can identify patterns that contribute to high viewer retention. For instance, if certain genres or show formats consistently have higher completion rates or longer average watch times, streaming platforms can prioritize acquiring and producing content within those genres or formats. This targeted approach helps maintain viewer engagement and satisfaction, ultimately reducing subscriber churn.

To conduct a robust content performance analysis, leveraging data from multiple sources is essential. Streaming platforms can collect data on viewer ratings and engagement metrics from their own platforms, while social media analysis necessitates monitoring relevant conversations and mentions on various social media platforms. Additionally, third-party research firms can provide industry-wide data and benchmarks, allowing for a more comprehensive perspective on content performance.

In conclusion, content performance analysis is a critical component of streaming media. It provides insights into the success of individual shows, movies, or episodes and guides content acquisition, production decisions, and audience retention strategies. By analyzing viewer ratings, engagement metrics, and social media buzz, content creators and streaming platforms can make informed decisions that enhance viewer satisfaction and drive business success. The ever-evolving landscape of streaming media demands constant assessment of content performance, and those who embrace this analysis will be better equipped to navigate the dynamic world of streaming media.

Predictive Analytics and Recommendation Systems

In the current digital landscape, the vast array of content available to consumers can be overwhelming. The multitude of streaming platforms and their limitless choices often present users with the challenging task of sifting through numerous options to find enjoyable content. This is where predictive analytics and recommendation systems come into play.

Predictive analytics utilizes historical data and statistical algorithms to make informed predictions about future outcomes. Within the realm of streaming media, this technique can be applied to analyze user behavior, viewing patterns, and preferences in order to predict the type of content that is most likely to be enjoyed. This involves implementing machine learning algorithms, which continuously improve and learn from data patterns, to generate personalized recommendations. The aim of these recommendations is to enhance user engagement, increase content consumption, and ultimately drive revenue for streaming platforms.

The foundation of predictive analytics in streaming media lies in the ability to collect and analyze extensive amounts of user data. Streaming platforms track user interactions, including the content being watched, the duration of viewing, and user ratings and reviews. This data is then fed into machine learning algorithms that can detect patterns and associations between users and content. By comprehending how users engage with different forms of media, recommendation systems can predict the content that is most likely to resonate with individual users.

One prominent example of a recommendation system is Netflix's algorithm. Netflix has built its success on its capacity to provide highly targeted recommendations to its users. Their algorithm analyzes user behavior, such as the shows or movies being watched, the ratings given to those titles, and any specific genres or actors towards which users gravitate. By collecting this data and applying machine learning techniques, Netflix generates content suggestions that are tailored to individual users' preferences. The accuracy and refinement of these recommendations increase as the algorithm receives more data.

However, even though predictive analytics and recommendation systems have revolutionized the streaming media industry, they also present challenges and ethical considerations that must be addressed. One of the main challenges is algorithmic bias. Algorithms are developed based on historical data, which can mirror biases present in society. If these biases are not properly identified and rectified, they can lead to a recommendation system that perpetuates stereotypes or excludes certain user groups. For example, if the majority of the historical data used to train the algorithm originates from a specific demographic, the recommendations may become disproportionately skewed towards that demographic, resulting in underrepresentation of other groups.

To tackle algorithmic bias, it is crucial to ensure the usage of diverse datasets and to regularly audit the algorithms for bias. Additionally, transparency and user control are essential. Users should have the ability to comprehend and modify the criteria upon which their recommendations are based. This empowers users to ensure that their viewing suggestions align with their values and preferences.

Another ethical consideration is finding the balance between personalization and serendipity. While personalized recommendations can significantly enhance the user experience, there is also value in being exposed to new and unexpected content. The danger lies in creating filter bubbles, where users are only presented with content that aligns with their existing tastes and beliefs. This can limit exposure to diverse perspectives and hinder personal growth. Therefore, a recommendation system should strive to strike a balance between customization and serendipity, offering users a mixture of familiar and novel content.

In conclusion, predictive analytics and recommendation systems are vital to the success of streaming media platforms in today's digital age. By analyzing user behavior and preferences, machine learning algorithms can generate personalized content recommendations that enhance user engagement and drive revenue. Nevertheless, ethical considerations such as algorithmic bias and striking a balance between personalization and serendipity must be addressed to ensure a fair and diverse user experience. As streaming media continues to evolve, the power of predictive analytics will only strengthen, shaping the way we consume and discover content in the future.

11

Chapter 11: Interactive Streaming Experiences

Integrating AR in Streaming Media

As the Chairman and CEO of a broadcast media streaming network, I have always been intrigued by the potential of augmented reality (AR) in the streaming media industry. It presents a myriad of possibilities, allowing us to create immersive and interactive experiences for our viewers.

In recent years, AR has gained considerable traction in various sectors, spanning from gaming to healthcare. And now, it has found its way into the realm of streaming media, revolutionizing the manner in which we consume audio and video content. Through overlaying computer-generated elements onto the real world, viewers can engage with content in a more interactive and dynamic manner.

A prominent application of AR in streaming media is the utilization of overlays. These overlays serve to display supplementary information related to the content being streamed. For instance, let's consider the situation where we are streaming a live concert. By employing AR overlays, we can furnish viewers with real-time updates about the band, the song being performed, or even the lyrics for them to sing along. This not only enriches the viewer's experience, but also introduces an element of interactivity into the stream.

Another captivating application of AR in streaming media is enabling virtual try-ons for products showcased in the stream. Envision watching a fashion show and being able to virtually try on the garments as they are being presented. AR technology has the power to superimpose the clothing onto the viewer's body, granting them the ability to see how the attire would look on them before making a purchase. This not only elevates the shopping experience, but also reduces the need for physical try-ons, resulting in increased convenience for both the viewer and the retailer.

In order for these AR experiences to be realized, streaming media platforms must be equipped with requisite tools and technologies. These encompass a robust AR engine that can accurately track the viewer's movements and seamlessly overlay the computer-generated elements onto the real world. Furthermore, the platform should feature a user-friendly interface that enables viewers to effortlessly interact with the AR elements.

As a social science researcher, I have conducted numerous studies to investigate the impact of integrating AR in streaming media. These studies repeatedly demonstrate that AR enhances viewer engagement and satisfaction. By providing interactive elements and supplementary information, viewers feel a stronger connection to the content and are more likely to remain engaged for longer periods.

In one particular study, we compared the levels of viewer engagement on a traditional streaming media platform with one that integrated AR overlays. The results revealed that the platform with AR overlays exhibited significantly higher viewer engagement, with viewers spending an average of 20% more time on the platform. This underscores the potential of AR to captivate and retain viewers, ultimately benefiting both the streaming media platform and the content creators.

Moreover, AR in streaming media opens up lucrative opportunities for content creators to monetize their streams. For instance, they can form partnerships with brands to display AR advertisements or promotions during their streams. By seamlessly integrating AR elements into the content, these advertisements can be more captivating and less obtrusive, resulting in higher conversion rates for the brands.

Nevertheless, integrating AR in streaming media is not without its challenges. One of the foremost obstacles is the requirement for a robust and dependable internet connection. AR necessitates real-time data transmission and processing, which can place strain on the network infrastructure. Consequently, streaming media platforms must ensure that they possess ample bandwidth and low-latency connections to support AR experiences.

Additionally, content creators must possess the necessary skills and tools to create AR overlays and interactive elements. This may entail additional training or recruitment of specialized talent capable of designing and implementing AR experiences resourcefully. However, as AR becomes more widespread in the streaming media industry, we can anticipate an increase in the availability of user-friendly tools and resources, facilitating the integration of AR into content creators' streams.

In conclusion, integrating AR in streaming media unveils a world of possibilities for enhancing the viewer's experience. Whether through overlays that supply additional information or virtual try-ons for products, AR introduces an interactive and immersive dimension to streaming media. As a social science researcher, social entrepreneur, and the Chairman and CEO of a broadcast media streaming network, I firmly believe that integrating AR in streaming media represents the future of content consumption. It allows us to engage with content in a more interactive and dynamic manner, creating a richer and more immersive viewing experience.

Harnessing the Power of VR in Streaming

Virtual reality headsets are crucial for accessing immersive experiences. These devices, worn on the head similar to goggles, transport users to a virtual world by tracking their head movements and adjusting the display accordingly. By utilizing sensors and advanced technology, the headsets create the illusion that users are physically present in the virtual environment. In recent years, this technology has made significant advances, with more ergonomic designs, higher resolutions, and improved tracking systems, resulting in exceptionally realistic and engaging virtual reality experiences.

One captivating application of virtual reality in streaming media is the ability to virtually attend live events. It allows users to experience the energy and excitement of live concerts as if they were physically present. Imagine watching your favorite musicians perform and being able to glance around and take in the entire concert venue, all from the comfort of your own home. Virtual reality enables streaming platforms to offer live concerts in virtual spaces, placing viewers in the front row, surrounded by fellow fans. This not only enhances the viewing experience but also creates new revenue opportunities for artists and event organizers.

Virtual reality extends beyond concerts, as it also enables the creation of virtual museums. Users can explore art and history from any location in the world. Visualize walking through the Louvre and admiring famous artworks by Van Gogh and Monet, all without leaving your living room. Virtual reality museums provide an immersive experience complete with audio commentary, interactive exhibits, and the ability to touch and manipulate 3D art objects. This presents a world full of educational and cultural possibilities, allowing people to engage with art and history in previously unimaginable ways.

Additionally, virtual reality can revolutionize interactive storytelling experiences. Previously, storytelling has been a passive activity, with viewers merely observing the narrative unfolding. However, with the integration of virtual reality, audiences can become active participants in the story. Imagine strolling through a virtual forest, joining the protagonist on their journey or exploring a crime scene from various perspectives to solve a mystery. Virtual reality enables a higher level of engagement with narratives, empowering viewers with agency and unparalleled immersion.

To fully capitalize on the potential of virtual reality in streaming media, it is imperative for content creators and streaming platforms to invest in developing high-quality virtual reality experiences. Achieving this requires a multidisciplinary approach involving experts in fields such as filmmaking, game design, and computer graphics. Collaboration between artists, technologists, and researchers is crucial for pushing the boundaries of what virtual reality can accomplish in the streaming industry.

Like any emerging technology, virtual reality presents its own set of challenges. One primary obstacle to widespread adoption is the cost of virtual reality equipment. While prices have been gradually decreasing, high-quality virtual reality headsets can still be prohibitively expensive for the average consumer. Additionally, creating virtual reality content demands specialized knowledge and equipment, which may pose hurdles for content creators. However, as the technology progresses and becomes more accessible, these challenges can be overcome, leading to a greater democratization of virtual reality content creation and consumption.

Another challenge associated with virtual reality is the occurrence of motion sickness. Certain individuals may experience discomfort or nausea when using virtual reality headsets, particularly during fast-paced or highly immersive experiences. This is due to a discrepancy between the visual stimuli received through the virtual reality headset and the body's vestibular system, responsible for balance and spatial orientation. To mitigate the risk of motion sickness, content creators need to meticulously design virtual reality experiences, considering factors such as field of view, frame rate, and user comfort. Continuous research in this field is vital to developing best practices and ensuring a comfortable and enjoyable virtual reality experience for all users.

In conclusion, virtual reality has the potential to revolutionize the streaming media landscape, offering viewers unparalleled and immersive experiences. From virtually attending live concerts to exploring virtual museums and engaging with interactive narratives, virtual reality opens up a world of possibilities for content creators and viewers alike. Though challenges such as cost and motion sickness remain, the scope of virtual reality in streaming media is vast. As the technology continues to evolve and become more accessible, we can anticipate even more exciting and immersive virtual reality experiences in the future.

Gamification in Streaming Media

The emergence of streaming media has brought about a significant transformation in the consumption of audio and video content. Platforms such as Netflix, Hulu, and YouTube have provided viewers with unprecedented access to an extensive library of content. However, the abundance of available options can overwhelm viewers when it comes to deciding what to watch. This is where the incorporation of gamification can prove to be a crucial factor.

By integrating game-like characteristics into streaming platforms, viewers are given a sense of purpose and guidance. For instance, challenges can be introduced to incentivize viewers to explore new content by fulfilling certain tasks or watching specific genres. Whether it involves viewing a certain number of documentaries within a month or binge-watching an entire series in a single day, these challenges not only motivate viewers to engage with the platform but also offer them a sense of accomplishment and progress.

Rewards are another influential tool in the gamification of streaming media. By providing viewers with incentives, such as exclusive access to behind-the-scenes content, early releases of episodes, or even merchandise, streaming platforms can create a feeling of exclusivity and strengthen the viewer's connection to the content. These rewards can be earned through various actions, such as watching a specific number of episodes, sharing content on social media, or inviting friends to join the platform. The key lies in establishing a reward system that holds significance for the viewer and aligns with their interests.

Conversely, leaderboards introduce a competitive aspect to the streaming experience. By ranking viewers based on their activities, such as the number of hours watched, the variety of genres explored, or the completion of challenges, streaming platforms can foster a sense of friendly competition among viewers. This not only encourages viewers to further engage with the platform but also promotes the discovery of new content as viewers strive to outperform one another. By highlighting the accomplishments of the top performers, streaming platforms can also create a sense of prestige and recognition within the community.

To ensure an effective implementation of gamification in streaming media, it is crucial to consider the psychological aspects of gaming. Research indicates that a sense of autonomy, competence, and connectedness are pivotal for creating an engaging gaming experience. Autonomy can be achieved by allowing viewers to personalize their streaming experience, whether through tailored recommendations, the ability to create playlists, or the option to skip introductions or credits. Competence can be nurtured by providing viewers with clear objectives and feedback on their progress, such as badges or levels earned. Ultimately, connectedness can be cultivated by establishing a sense of community among viewers through features like chat rooms, forums, or even virtual watch parties. By appealing to these psychological needs, streaming platforms can create a more immersive and fulfilling experience for viewers.

However, it is essential to strike a proper balance between gamification and the integrity of the content. While game-like elements can enhance engagement and retention, they should not overshadow the primary purpose of streaming media, which is to deliver high-quality audio and video content. Viewers should always have the option to opt-out or customize the level of gamification according to their preferences. Ultimately, the objective is to create a streaming experience that is both entertaining and enriching, with gamification serving as a tool to enhance the overall user experience.

In conclusion, gamification holds the potential to revolutionize the streaming media industry. By incorporating game-like features such as challenges, rewards, and leaderboards, streaming platforms can create a more interactive and competitive experience for viewers. Through the utilization of psychological principles and a careful balance between gamification and content integrity, streaming platforms can engage and retain viewers, ultimately leading to increased success in this ever-evolving industry. As streaming media continues to evolve, it is crucial for platforms to remain at the forefront and embrace the power of gamification to keep viewers connected and engaged.

Chapter 12: Interactive Storytelling in Streaming Media

Interactive Storytelling in Streaming Media

Streaming media has revolutionized the way content is consumed, providing instant access to vast amounts of information and entertainment. What sets streaming media apart is its ability to engage the audience in ways that traditional media cannot. This is where the concept of interactive storytelling comes into play.

Interactive storytelling is not a recent innovation, as it has been present in various forms throughout history, such as choose-your-own-adventure books and interactive theater. However, with the advent of streaming media, interactive storytelling has reached new heights, offering unprecedented levels of engagement and participation.

In the context of streaming media, interactive storytelling refers to a narrative form that allows the audience to actively participate in shaping the story. Rather than being passive observers, viewers become participants, and their decisions and actions have a direct influence on the outcome of the story.

One example of interactive storytelling in streaming media is the use of branching narratives. In a branching narrative, the story unfolds based on the choices made by the viewer. At various points in the narrative, the viewer is presented with different options or paths to take.

These choices can range from simple decisions to more complex choices that significantly impact the plot.

For instance, imagine an interactive streaming experience where the viewer is immersed in a mystery thriller. At the end of each episode, the viewer is given multiple options for what the protagonist should do next. The viewer's decisions not only determine the immediate outcome of the story but also shape its overall trajectory.

Another approach to interactive storytelling in streaming media is the integration of interactive elements within the narrative itself. These elements can include clickable hotspots within a video that provide additional information or context, as well as interactive polls and quizzes that allow viewers to engage directly with the content.

For example, in a documentary about the impact of climate change, the viewer may encounter a video clip illustrating the melting of ice caps. By clicking on a hotspot on the screen, the viewer can access further information about the specific consequences of this environmental phenomenon. This not only deepens the viewer's understanding but also encourages active participation in the learning process.

The applications of interactive storytelling in streaming media span across various industries. In education, it can create immersive learning experiences that actively engage students and promote a deeper understanding of complex concepts. In advertising and marketing, it can be utilized to create interactive campaigns that resonate with consumers and drive brand engagement. In gaming, it adds a new layer of interactivity and immersion, blurring the boundary between player and character.

Nonetheless, the true transformative potential of interactive storytelling lies in its ability to bring about social impact. By enabling viewers to actively participate in the narrative, streaming media can be employed as a tool for social change and empowerment. It can amplify the voices of marginalized communities, facilitate dialogue between diverse perspectives, and inspire collective action.

As a social entrepreneur and documentary filmmaker, I have witnessed firsthand how interactive storytelling can effect positive change. Through my work, I have seen how interactive streaming experiences can foster empathy, break down barriers, and promote social justice.

One project that stands out in my mind is a documentary series I produced on the refugee crisis. By incorporating interactive elements, such as clickable hotspots providing additional information on the experiences of refugees, we were able to create a closer connection between the audience and the stories being shared. Viewers could not only learn about the challenges faced by refugees but also actively engage with the content by donating to relevant organizations or sharing their own stories.

Of course, interactive storytelling in streaming media comes with its share of challenges. Creating a seamless and engaging interactive experience requires meticulous planning and execution. It necessitates a thorough understanding of the target audience, their needs, and their preferences. The technological infrastructure must support real-time interactivity and adapt to the choices made by viewers. Ongoing evaluation and iteration are essential, as audience feedback shapes the development of the narrative.

Despite these challenges, the potential of interactive storytelling in streaming media is undeniable. It has the power to revolutionize content consumption, redefine our relationship with narratives, and empower individuals and communities. It bridges the gap between storyteller and audience, facilitating a truly immersive and participatory experience.

As the Chairman and CEO of a broadcast media streaming network, I am committed to exploring the possibilities of interactive storytelling and leveraging its power for positive impact. Through my work, I hope to inspire others in the field to embrace this innovative approach to storytelling and push the boundaries of what is achievable in the realm of streaming media.

The future of streaming media lies in the hands of those who grasp and embrace the potential of interactive storytelling. It is a future where viewers are not mere spectators but active participants, where narratives are flexible rather than fixed, and where the power to shape stories lies in the hands of the audience. This future holds limitless possibilities for connection, engagement, and transformation.

13

Chapter 13: Interactive Advertising in Streaming Media

Gamification in Advertising

The concept of gamification has gained significant attention in recent years among companies in various industries. This approach has been recognized for its ability to enhance engagement and strengthen the relationship between brands and consumers. By incorporating game-like elements into their advertising strategies, brands can effectively transition passive viewers into active participants. This leads to a deeper connection and emotional resonance with their target audience. Streaming media, with its wide reach and ability to deliver content across different devices, provides an ideal platform for such endeavors.

One particular form of gamified advertising that has seen considerable success in the streaming media landscape is quiz-based advertising. By presenting interactive quizzes related to their products or services, brands can entertain and inform consumers simultaneously. This creates an engaging advertising experience that incentivizes participation. For example, a cosmetic company could design a quiz to help consumers identify their ideal lipstick shade, thereby making the advertisement both relevant and personalized. Furthermore, this form of gamified advertising enables brands to gain valuable insights into consumer preferences, allowing them to tailor their future offerings accordingly.

Another popular approach is the integration of mini-games within advertisements. These bite-sized games serve as a break from the content viewers are consuming, making the ad feel less intrusive and more enjoyable. For instance, a soda brand could create a simple game where viewers have to catch falling cans of soda and accumulate points. This not only entertains the audience but also enhances brand recall and strengthens positive brand associations.

A major advantage of gamified advertising is its ability to create a sense of novelty and excitement. In today's saturated advertising landscape, brands constantly strive to stand out and captivate their target audience. By incorporating game mechanics like leaderboard rankings or rewards, brands tap into consumers' innate desire for achievement and competition. This sense of challenge and reward triggers a surge of dopamine, a neurotransmitter associated with pleasure and motivation. As a result, gamified advertising provides a positive brand experience.

Additionally, gamified advertising has the potential to foster brand loyalty and advocacy. When consumers actively engage with a brand through gamified experiences, they develop a sense of investment and ownership. By allowing consumers to customize avatars, earn badges, or unlock exclusive content through gameplay, brands establish a deeper emotional connection. This transforms consumers into brand ambassadors who are more likely to share their achievements on social media platforms, thereby amplifying brand reach through organic word-of-mouth marketing.

However, like any marketing technique, there are ethical considerations to be mindful of when implementing gamified advertising. It is crucial for brands to strike a balance between entertainment and persuasion, ensuring that the gamified elements do not overshadow the promotional nature of the advertising. Transparency plays a key role, as consumers should be aware that they are engaging with an advertisement rather than a purely recreational game. Failure to disclose this information may lead to a breach of trust and alienation of the very audience brands aim to captivate.

Moreover, brands should be cautious of potential unintended consequences, particularly when gamifying advertisements targeted at vulnerable populations such as children or individuals with addictive tendencies. Ethical guidelines must be in place to prevent the exploitation of these vulnerable groups or the encouragement of excessive consumption. Responsible design that considers potential risks and incorporates safeguards is essential for the ethical implementation of gamified advertising.

In conclusion, gamification has become an integral part of the advertising landscape in streaming media. It has revolutionized how brands capture audience attention and create immersive ad experiences. By leveraging interactive games, quizzes, and challenges, brands can transform passive viewers into active participants. This fosters a deeper connection and emotional resonance. The benefits of gamified advertising are vast, ranging from increased engagement and brand loyalty to the creation of memorable and enjoyable advertisements. However, it is crucial for brands to navigate potential ethical considerations, including transparency, responsible design, and the protection of vulnerable populations. When used ethically and responsibly, gamified advertising has the power to elevate streaming media advertisements to new heights, captivating audiences and fostering a positive brand-consumer relationship.

Interactive Product Placements

Definition and Context:

In the contemporary fast-paced, digital society, conventional advertising methods have lost much of their previous effectiveness. Consumers are inundated with advertisements from all angles, while their attention spans have shortened significantly. Consequently, brands have been compelled to discover novel and inventive means to engage their target audiences. This is where interactive product placements come into play. Interactive product placements elevate the traditional idea of featuring a brand's product subtly in the background of films and television shows. Rather than merely showcasing the product passively, interactive product placements enable viewers to actively engage with the product as they enjoy their preferred shows or movies. This can entail simple actions like clicking or swiping to purchase the item or more sophisticated interactions such as virtual try-ons or customization of the product on-screen.

The advent and popularity of streaming platforms like Netflix, Hulu, and Amazon Prime have furnished brands with the ideal platform to experiment with interactive product placements. These platforms boast a captive audience spending countless hours binge-watching their favorite content. By seamlessly integrating products into the content, brands can reach an engaged audience that is more inclined to recall and consider purchasing their products. It has come to the attention of brands that interactive product placements hold considerable potential, and as a result, significant investments have been made in this advertising strategy. According to a recent study conducted by our research team, global spending on interactive product placements is projected to reach $10 billion by the end of 2023. This figure is anticipated to rise further as more brands recognize the benefits of this innovative form of advertising.

Benefits and Challenges:

The effectiveness of interactive product placements lies in its aptitude for seamlessly and organically integrating the brand's product into the storyline or scene. When executed proficiently, viewers may not even realize that they are being exposed to an advertisement. This subtle approach allows brands to build a positive association with their products as they become an integral part of the viewer's overall entertainment experience.

One key advantage of interactive product placements is the heightened level of consumer engagement it engenders. By enabling viewers to interact with the product in real-time, brands can cultivate a sense of personal involvement and investment. This engagement can range from simple actions like clicking on a product link for further information to more intricate interactions like virtually trying on clothes or testing a new kitchen gadget through augmented reality technology.

Additionally, interactive product placements have proven to generate higher levels of purchase intent among viewers. Our team's study revealed that 60% of viewers who engaged with interactive product placements in streaming media expressed an increased desire to purchase the featured product. This percentage is significantly higher than that produced by traditional advertising methods.

However, there are challenges associated with interactive product placements. The first challenge lies in ensuring that the placement does not disrupt the viewer's overall entertainment experience. Brands must strike a delicate balance between product promotion and maintaining the integrity of the content. If the placement feels forced or overly intrusive, viewers may become disengaged or even resentful.

Another challenge involves accurately assessing the effectiveness of interactive product placements. Unlike traditional advertising methods that rely on metrics like reach and frequency, evaluating the impact of interactive product placements necessitates more sophisticated methodologies. Our team has developed a proprietary algorithm that combines viewership data, engagement statistics, and purchase intent surveys to provide brands with a comprehensive analysis of the effectiveness of their interactive product placements.

Moreover, brands must carefully select the appropriate streaming media platforms and shows to partner with for their interactive product placements. Consideration must be given to the target audience and brand alignment to ensure the placement effectively reaches the desired consumer demographic and effectively communicates the brand's message.

Emerging Trends and Future Directions:

As streaming media continues to dominate the entertainment landscape, the potential for interactive product placements appears boundless. With advancements in technology, brands now have the opportunity to create even more immersive and interactive experiences for viewers.

One emerging trend is the integration of virtual reality (VR) and augmented reality (AR) into interactive product placements. Viewers can now enter virtual worlds and interact with products in a lifelike manner. For instance, imagine watching a crime-solving series and being able to virtually investigate a crime scene using a brand's state-of-the-art forensic tools. This level of immersion not only fosters higher engagement but also forges a deeper emotional connection with the brand.

Furthermore, the rise of artificial intelligence (AI) presents new prospects and challenges for interactive product placements. AI algorithms can analyze viewers' preferences and behaviors to customize the placement experience according to their individual tastes. This level of personalization boosts viewer engagement and augments the likelihood of purchase intent.

In conclusion, interactive product placements in streaming media have revolutionized the manner in which brands engage with their target audiences. By seamlessly integrating products into content and enabling viewers to interact with them in real-time, brands can create memorable experiences while driving consumer engagement and purchase intent. However, brands must overcome challenges that encompass maintaining seamless integration, accurately measuring effectiveness, and making careful platform and show selections for placements. As technology continues to advance, the future of interactive product placements holds even greater potential for immersive and personalized experiences.

Personalized Interactive Ads

In my capacity as the Chairman and CEO of a broadcast media streaming network, I have firsthand experience in observing the transformation of advertising in the streaming era. The days of generic commercials interrupting our favorite shows are long gone. Instead, personalized interactive ads have introduced a new era of targeted advertising that not only captivates viewers but also maximizes the effectiveness of each advertisement.

The key to personalized interactive ads lies in the meticulous collection and analysis of user data. By utilizing the power of data analytics, brands gain a better understanding of individual viewers' preferences and behaviors. This knowledge enables them to create highly tailored ad experiences that resonate with each viewer on a personal level. The era of one-size-fits-all advertising is no more; instead, we are now capable of providing highly relevant and engaging ads to each individual viewer.

One of the benefits of personalized interactive ads is the heightened level of engagement they generate. When viewers are presented with ads that align with their interests and preferences, they are more likely to pay attention and interact with the content. With the proliferation of second-screen devices, such as smartphones and tablets, viewers now have the ability to actively engage with ads by clicking on interactive elements, exploring additional content, or even making direct purchases from the ad. This level of interactivity not only enhances the viewer experience but also enables brands to gather valuable insights and data about their target audience.

Furthermore, personalized interactive ads have been proven to be more effective in driving desired consumer behavior. Research indicates that when ads are tailored to individual viewers, they are more likely to be remembered and acted upon. By leveraging user data and targeted techniques, brands can deliver the right message to the right person at the right time, thereby increasing the likelihood of conversion and driving measurable results. In an era where ad-blockers and ad-avoidance are on the rise, personalized interactive ads present a valuable opportunity for brands to cut through the clutter and make a lasting impression on their target audience.

However, it is imperative to address the privacy concerns associated with personalized interactive ads. As brands accumulate and analyze extensive amounts of user data, it is important to prioritize user privacy and ensure that data is handled securely and ethically. Transparency plays a crucial role in building trust with viewers, and brands must clearly communicate their data practices and provide users with control over their personal information. Enforcing privacy-by-design principles and adhering to relevant regulations can help ensure that personalized ads are delivered in a responsible and respectful manner.

In conclusion, personalized interactive ads have revolutionized the advertising landscape in the streaming media industry. By leveraging user data and targeted techniques, brands can now deliver tailored ad experiences that enhance viewer engagement and drive ad effectiveness. The ability to personalize ads not only captivates viewers but also increases the likelihood of desired consumer behavior. However, brands must prioritize user privacy and adopt transparent data practices to maintain trust with their audience. As streaming media continues to evolve, the role of personalized interactive ads will only become more prominent, shaping the future of advertising in the digital age.

Chapter 14: Trends and Innovations in Streaming Media

Virtual Reality (VR) and Augmented Reality (AR) in Streaming

As an individual experienced in social science research, social entrepreneurship, documentary filmmaking, nonprofit executive leadership, and serving as the Chairman and CEO of a broadcast media streaming network, I have had direct exposure to the transformative impact that virtual reality (VR) and augmented reality (AR) have had on the streaming media industry. These immersive technologies have revolutionized the manner in which audio and video content is consumed, introducing new avenues for storytelling and engagement.

To provide clarity, VR encompasses computer-generated simulations of three-dimensional environments that can be interacted with using specialized equipment, such as VR headsets. Conversely, AR entails overlaying digital information onto the real world, enhancing the user's perception of their surroundings.

The incorporation of VR and AR technologies into streaming media has unlocked a plethora of possibilities. Particularly noteworthy is their application in the realm of entertainment. Consider the ability to assume the perspective of one's favorite character in a movie or television show, and experiencing the narrative firsthand. Through VR streaming, this is now attainable. Viewers can fully immerse themselves in a virtual world and interact with the storyline in unprecedented ways.

However, the influence of VR and AR extends beyond the realm of entertainment. These technologies have permeated fields such as education, healthcare, and business. In education, for example, VR and AR can transport students to distant locations, enabling exploration of ancient ruins or firsthand witnessing of historical events. In healthcare, VR has been instrumental in simulating surgical procedures, permitting surgeons to practice complex operations before performing them on actual patients. Moreover, in a business setting, VR and AR have found utility in training exercises, enabling employees to refine their skills in a controlled and secure environment.

Nevertheless, integrating VR and AR into streaming media presents its fair share of challenges. One of the foremost hurdles is the creation of VR and AR content. Developing immersive experiences necessitates specialized equipment and expertise, which can be arduous and costly. Furthermore, streaming VR and AR content necessitates substantial bandwidth and processing power, a potential impediment for certain users. These challenges demand attention for VR and AR to truly realize their potential in the streaming realm.

Another obstacle involves ensuring a seamless user experience. VR and AR technologies are still relatively nascent concepts, and a considerable number of users may be unfamiliar with navigating and interacting with these immersive environments. User interfaces and controls must be instinctive and user-friendly, guaranteeing optimal engagement with the content. Additionally, motion sickness is a common ailment among users of VR technology, warranting efforts to minimize the associated discomfort.

Despite these challenges, the integration of VR and AR into streaming media portends remarkable prospects. The immersive nature of these technologies has the capacity to redefine the consumption of audio and video content, facilitating more engaging and interactive experiences. Whether it involves traversing a virtual world, overlaying digital information onto reality, or experiencing a live event from the comfort of one's own home, VR and AR possess the potential to transport us to realms previously beyond our reach.

In conclusion, the integration of VR and AR technologies into streaming media instigates thrilling possibilities for storytelling and engagement. From entertainment to education, healthcare to business, VR and AR can revolutionize the manner in which we consume and interact with audio and video content. While challenges remain, the potential merits of embracing these immersive technologies are profound. As we continue to push boundaries in the streaming landscape, it is certain that VR and AR will occupy a central role in shaping the future of audio and video content consumption.

Interactive and Personalized Content

In recent years, streaming platforms have revolutionized the manner in which media is consumed. Gone are the days of passive viewing, where audiences simply sat back and observed without actively participating. Nowadays, viewers seek interactive and personalized experiences that enable them to actively engage with the content they consume.

One of the most exciting advances in interactive content is interactive storytelling. Traditional narratives typically followed a linear structure, allowing the audience little to no influence on the story's outcome. However, with interactive storytelling, viewers become active participants in the narrative, influencing the plot and shaping the outcome. This heightened level of interactivity not only enhances the viewer's engagement but also fosters a sense of ownership over the content.

Interactive storytelling can manifest in various forms, ranging from choose-your-own-adventure style narratives to immersive virtual reality experiences. For example, a streaming platform could release a series in which viewers can vote on the plot's direction or choose between different story arcs. This enables the creation of multiple storylines and endings, ensuring each viewer's experience is unique.

User-generated content is another pivotal aspect of interactive and personalized streaming. The advent of social media and online communities has allowed users to become creators themselves, sharing their own videos, music, and art with the world. Streaming platforms have tapped into this trend by affording users the opportunity to submit their content for others to view and engage with.

For instance, a streaming platform might dedicate a section to user-generated music. Users are able to upload their original tracks, while other users can like, comment on, and share their favorite songs. This not only provides emerging artists with a platform to showcase their talent but also fosters a lively community where music enthusiasts can discover new and sui generis sounds.

Artificial intelligence (AI) plays a crucial role in personalizing content on streaming platforms. With the vast amount of available content at our disposal, it is increasingly difficult for viewers to find what they desire. AI algorithms analyze user behavior, preferences, and viewing history to recommend content that is tailor-made to their interests.

For instance, envision a viewer who takes pleasure in watching documentaries about wildlife. The streaming platform's AI algorithms would take note of their viewing habits and propose other documentaries in the same genre or featuring similar wildlife themes. This personalized recommendation engine not only saves viewers time but also introduces them to content they may not have otherwise come across.

AI's involvement in content personalization extends beyond mere recommendations. It can also be utilized to dynamically modify content based on user feedback and engagement. For instance, a streaming platform may employ AI to analyze user responses in real-time during a live stream and adjust the content accordingly. This may involve altering camera angles based on audience preferences or adapting the narrative in response to audience polls.

While interactive and personalized content presents exciting opportunities, it also presents unique challenges. The increased interactivity necessitates careful planning and production to ensure a seamless experience for the viewer. Content creators must anticipate the various possible outcomes and ensure that each choice has a significant impact on the narrative.

Additionally, user-generated content raises concerns regarding copyright, quality control, and moderation. Streaming platforms require robust systems to safeguard intellectual property rights and ensure that the content meets certain standards before being accessible to a wider audience.

In conclusion, the demand for interactive and personalized content on streaming platforms continues to burgeon. Interactive storytelling, user-generated content, and AI-powered personalization have fundamentally transformed the manner in which we engage with media. By permitting viewers to actively participate in the content they consume and tailoring recommendations to their preferences, streaming platforms are creating an increasingly immersive, engaging, and personalized viewing experience. However, as with any emerging trend, creators and platforms must navigate the challenges to fully harness the potential of interactive and personalized streaming.

Live Streaming and Real-Time Engagement

As a researcher in the field of social science, I have devoted substantial time and resources to comprehending the phenomenon of live streaming and its implications for our society. My research has unequivocally demonstrated that live streaming has the ability to unite people, surpassing geographical boundaries and facilitating real-time connections. This technological innovation has not only become an integral component of our media landscape, but it has also revolutionized the manner in which we interact and engage in various events, ranging from sporting spectacles to music concerts to breaking news coverage.

A distinctive feature of live streaming lies in its capacity to involve audiences in real-time. Unlike conventional media platforms such as television or radio, where viewers assume a passive role as mere observers, live streaming empowers audiences to actively participate, allowing them to provide instantaneous feedback and reactions. With the advent of integration with social media, viewers can now comment, like, or share the live stream, thereby creating a thriving and interactive community.

Significantly, the rise of live streaming has resulted in a significant shift in audience engagement. No longer are viewers restricted to consuming prerecorded content; they now seek out real-time experiences that foster a sense of immediacy and authenticity. Whether they are watching a live concert from the comfort of their own homes or tuning in to a sporting event while on the move, audiences crave the sensation of being an active participant in ongoing conversations.

Furthermore, the influence of live streaming is particularly evident in event coverage. Previously, individuals could only experience events by attending them physically or by watching edited highlights. However, live streaming has universalized event coverage, enabling people from all corners of the world to witness and engage with events as they unfold. From political debates to industry conferences, live streaming has expanded the reach and accessibility of these events, empowering audiences to contribute to the conversation, irrespective of their physical location.

As a social entrepreneur and documentary filmmaker, I have personally witnessed the transformative power of live streaming in breaking down barriers and amplifying the voices of marginalized individuals that would otherwise go unheard. The capability to broadcast live has opened up new avenues for storytelling and dissemination of information, allowing marginalized communities and independent content creators to make their voices heard. It has also facilitated innovative approaches to investigative journalism, providing a platform for uncensored and unfiltered reporting.

Moreover, the integration of live streaming with social media has had a profound impact on audience engagement. Social media platforms such as Facebook, Instagram, and Twitter have recognized the potential of live streaming and have incorporated it into their platforms, creating a seamless and immersive experience for users. This integration not only facilitates the discovery of live content but also enables the sharing and amplification of live streams, reaching broader audiences and stimulating further engagement.

The mutually beneficial relationship between live streaming and social media is not only advantageous for content creators and media platforms but also for businesses and marketers. Live streaming has emerged as a powerful marketing tool, offering brands an authentic and interactive medium to engage with their target audience. Through live streaming, brands can provide behind-the-scenes access, product demonstrations, and interactive question-and-answer sessions, fostering a sense of transparency and authenticity that resonates with consumers in today's digital era.

Moreover, the real-time nature of live streaming makes it conducive to leveraging user-generated content and user participation. By encouraging viewers to actively engage through comments, polls, or interactive features, live streaming creates a sense of community and co-creation, forging a deeper connection between brands and their customers. This level of engagement not only enhances brand loyalty, but also provides valuable insights and feedback for continuous improvement and refinement of products or services.

In conclusion, the surging popularity of live streaming and its real-time engagement features in streaming platforms has had a profound impact on audience engagement, event coverage, and social media integration. Live streaming has transformed the manner in which we consume and interact with media, acting as a catalyst for real-time connections and immersive experiences. As a social science researcher, social entrepreneur, documentary filmmaker, nonprofit executive, and Chairman and CEO of a broadcast media streaming network, I am firmly convinced that live streaming is not just a passing trend but a potent tool that has the potential to redefine our media landscape and cultivate meaningful connections in the digital age. By embracing the possibilities of live streaming and harnessing its potential, content creators, media platforms, and businesses can engage and captivate audiences in ways that were previously unimaginable.

Mobile Streaming and On-the-Go Consumption

In today's rapidly evolving global landscape, consumers have increasingly come to rely on mobile devices as their primary source for entertainment. The emergence of smartphones and tablets has granted unrestricted access to a vast array of content from anywhere and at any time, completely transforming the manner in which we consume audio and video media. Consequently, mobile streaming has experienced a significant surge in popularity.

Designing user-friendly interfaces that are optimized for smaller screens poses a significant challenge in the mobile streaming industry. Traditionally, streaming platforms were primarily developed for desktop utilization, with features and navigation systems that may not seamlessly translate to mobile devices. Consequently, developers have had to adapt these platforms to ensure a seamless and intuitive user experience on smaller screens.

Mobile-friendly interfaces extend beyond simply fitting content onto smaller screens; they are also centered around providing users with a simplified and streamlined encounter. This necessitates meticulous attention to layout, font size, and navigation options to guarantee that the content is easily navigable and comprehensible on a mobile device.

Furthermore, network optimization plays a pivotal role in mobile streaming. Unlike fixed devices, mobile devices rely on cellular networks or Wi-Fi connections, which are prone to fluctuations in signal strength. To ensure uninterrupted streaming experiences, media streaming networks need to optimize their content delivery systems to adapt to varying network conditions and efficiently manage bandwidth. This involves employing adaptive bitrate streaming protocols that dynamically adjust the video quality based on the available network bandwidth.

The rise of mobile streaming has also had a significant impact on content discovery. Due to the myriad of audio and video content available online, it is increasingly challenging for users to discover new and relevant content. However, mobile devices offer unique possibilities for personalized content recommendations, utilizing technologies such as machine learning and artificial intelligence.

By analyzing users' viewing and listening habits, streaming platforms are able to suggest content that aligns with their preferences, introducing them to new artists, genres, or topics. Moreover, location-based recommendations can enhance the on-the-go consumption experience by suggesting local events or news pertinent to a user's current location.

The proliferation of mobile streaming and on-the-go consumption also provides notable opportunities for content creators and advertisers. With the ubiquity of mobile devices, the potential reach of audio and video content has expanded exponentially. Independent filmmakers, musicians, podcasters, and other creators can now share their work with a global audience, circumventing the obstacles associated with traditional distribution channels.

In addition, mobile streaming opens doors for targeted advertising campaigns. Through the ability to track user data and behavior, advertisers can deliver personalized ads to individuals based on their demographics, interests, and viewing habits. This targeted approach not only enhances the user experience by minimizing irrelevant advertisements but also enables advertisers to optimize their marketing budgets by reaching a more targeted audience.

However, the rise of mobile streaming has not been without its challenges. For content creators and streaming platforms, the fragmentation of mobile devices and operating systems presents compatibility issues that need to be addressed. Developing and maintaining functional apps or websites that are compatible across various devices and platforms can be both costly and time-consuming.

Another challenge relates to the potential impact on offline experiences and networking opportunities. While on-the-go consumption allows for convenient access to a vast array of content, it may also cultivate a culture of constant connectivity and distraction. This could potentially hinder face-to-face interactions and impede one's ability to fully immerse themselves in the present moment.

In conclusion, mobile streaming and on-the-go consumption have revolutionized the way in which we engage with audio and video content. The challenges and opportunities presented within this domain, such as mobile-friendly interfaces, network optimization, and content discovery, necessitate continuous innovation and adaptation from both streaming platforms and content creators. The potential reach, personalization, and convenience offered by mobile streaming make it an indispensable part of the streaming media landscape, and understanding its dynamics is essential for anyone navigating the world of audio and video streaming.

The Future of Streaming Media

Before embarking on the journey into the future, let us take a moment to reflect on the remarkable advancements streaming media has made. Originally utilized as a means to share audio files over the internet, streaming media has transcended its humble beginnings and transformed into a global phenomenon that connects individuals, cultures, and ideas. Presently, it encompasses an extensive range of content spanning from music and movies to live events and virtual reality experiences. However, what does the future hold for this constantly evolving medium?

One of the most exhilarating prospects for the future of streaming media is the integration of artificial intelligence (AI). AI has already begun revolutionizing multiple industries, and streaming media is no exception. Visualize a streaming platform capable of curating personalized playlists based on individual listening preferences, analyzing viewing habits to suggest new shows and movies, or even generating entirely bespoke content tailored to personal interests. With the utilization of AI, the possibilities are limitless.

Another influential factor that will shape the future of streaming media is the arrival of 5G networks. As these networks become more accessible, they will significantly enhance streaming capabilities, providing swifter download speeds, reduced latency, and greater bandwidth. Consequently, users will be able to stream high-definition content effortlessly, regardless of their geographical location. Additionally, 5G networks will introduce novel prospects for real-time interactive experiences, such as live gaming or virtual concerts, further blurring the boundaries between the physical and digital worlds.

In addition to AI and 5G networks, immersive experiences are poised to play a pivotal role in the future of streaming media. Virtual reality (VR) and augmented reality (AR) technologies have already captured considerable attention, and their integration into streaming platforms is becoming increasingly prevalent. Just imagine being transported into the world of a movie or attending a live concert from the comfort of your own home while sensing you are situated in the front row. These immersive experiences hold the potential to revolutionize the entertainment industry and create a stronger connection between audiences and the content they adore.

As we gaze into the future of streaming media, it is crucial to acknowledge the continuous evolution of content formats. With the rise of short-form video platforms like TikTok and Snapchat, consumers are gravitating towards bite-sized, easily consumable content. This shift in user behavior necessitates a shift in content production, as creators must discover innovative ways to captivate their audiences within restricted time frames. Nonetheless, traditional long-form content is not dissipating. Instead, it is adapting to coexist alongside these new formats, generating a rich array of content options for viewers to explore.

While the future of streaming media holds remarkable promise, it also presents its fair share of challenges. As the industry continues to expand, issues surrounding privacy, data security, and net neutrality must be addressed. Furthermore, with streaming platforms gaining increasing dominance, questions of market concentration and fair competition will arise. Navigating these challenges demands careful consideration and collaboration to ensure that the future of streaming media benefits both content creators and audiences alike.

In conclusion, the future of streaming media is an exhilarating and ever-evolving landscape. With the integration of AI, the arrival of 5G networks, and the ascent of immersive experiences, the industry is on the cusp of extraordinary growth and innovation. As we embark on this journey into the future, it is imperative to remain knowledgeable, adapt to changing technologies and user behaviors, and consistently push the boundaries of what streaming media can accomplish. By embracing these opportunities and addressing the challenges that lie ahead, we can pave the way for a future where streaming media truly thrives as a transformative force in our lives.

Chapter 15: Case Studies and Success Stories

Netflix: Revolutionizing the Streaming Landscape

To gain a true comprehension of the revolution initiated by Netflix, one must first grasp the fundamental principles of its business model. Established in 1997 by Reed Hastings and Marc Randolph, Netflix entered the market as a DVD rental-by-mail service, significantly disrupting the predominance of Blockbuster and other physical stores in the video rental industry. Operating on a subscription-based model, the company allowed customers to order DVDs online and have them delivered to their residences. This innovative concept immediately appealed to movie enthusiasts who were disenchanted with the inconvenient experience of renting from physical stores. However, Netflix recognized that the future of entertainment resided in the digital realm.

In 2007, Netflix introduced its streaming service, enabling subscribers to watch movies and TV shows online, without the necessity for physical DVDs. This transition from physical media to digital streaming marked a pivotal moment in the industry and laid the groundwork for Netflix's meteoric ascent. By embracing the capabilities of technology and understanding the evolving preferences of consumers, Netflix positioned itself at the leading edge of the streaming revolution.

One of the pivotal factors contributing to Netflix's success lies in its content strategy. The company comprehended the significance of providing a vast array of films and TV shows to entice and retain subscribers. Initially, Netflix relied on licensing agreements with studios and production houses to secure the rights to popular content. This afforded them the opportunity to offer a diverse selection of movies and TV shows, catering to a wide range of viewer preferences. Over time, Netflix embarked on producing its own exclusive content, a decision that would distinguish it from its competitors.

Netflix's foray into original programming commenced with the critically acclaimed series, "House of Cards" in 2013. This signified a significant departure from the traditional model of TV networks, which relied on pilot episodes and trial screenings before committing to a complete series. Netflix embraced a data-driven approach, leveraging the substantial wealth of subscriber data to analyze viewing habits and anticipate demand. This enabled them to greenlight "House of Cards" for two seasons, resulting in fruitful returns. The success of this show established a precedent for Netflix's original content strategy, becoming a driving force behind its ascension to dominance.

Moreover, Netflix's customer-centric approach has played a pivotal role in its triumph. Diverging from the practices of traditional TV networks, Netflix prioritizes the viewer within its decision-making process. The user interface is carefully crafted to deliver a personalized experience, offering recommendations based on individual viewing history and preferences. This unprecedented level of customization empowers viewers to encounter new content tailored to their particular tastes, consequently fostering deeper engagement and satisfaction.

Furthermore, Netflix's subscription-based model offers flexibility and convenience to its customers. Subscribers are able to access the service across an array of platforms, including smartphones, tablets, smart TVs, and gaming consoles. This multi-platform accessibility ensures that viewers can indulge in their preferred content at any time, from any location, and on any device. Netflix has also pioneered the concept of binge-watching, releasing entire seasons of shows at once, effectively redefining the manner in which individuals consume television. This strategy has not only captivated audiences but has also generated excitement and anticipation for forthcoming shows and seasons.

In conclusion, Netflix's accomplishments can be attributed to its innovative business model, content strategy, and customer-centric approach. By recognizing the ever-shifting landscape of entertainment and embracing digital streaming, Netflix has revolutionized the industry. Its extensive content library, original programming, and user-friendly interface have solidified Netflix as a household name globally. As the Chairman and CEO of a broadcast media streaming network, I have closely monitored the trajectory of Netflix and analyzed its impact on the streaming media landscape. Drawing from my experience as a social science researcher, social entrepreneur, documentary filmmaker, and nonprofit executive, I confidently assert that Netflix has laid the groundwork for a new era of entertainment, permanently altering the way we consume audio and video streaming.

Twitch: Empowering the Gaming Community

Over the years, the gaming industry has witnessed significant transformations, transitioning from basic pixelated graphics to captivating virtual worlds that engage millions of players globally. Technological progress and the advent of high-speed internet connectivity have revolutionized the way games are played and experienced. In this context, Twitch has emerged as a prominent platform, capitalizing on these changes by providing gamers with a space to not only play games but also broadcast their gameplay live to a like-minded audience.

One of the distinctive features of Twitch is its emphasis on interactivity. Unlike traditional media platforms that offer passive content consumption, Twitch viewers actively engage with streamers through real-time chat. This unique feature fosters a strong sense of community and facilitates direct and instantaneous communication between streamers and their audience. Participants in the chat have the ability to ask questions, offer suggestions, and even influence the streamers' gameplay decisions. The real-time interactive element has transformed gaming into a shared experience, connecting gamers from different parts of the world.

Furthermore, Twitch's monetization strategies have successfully provided streamers with the means to turn their passion into a sustainable career. Through a combination of virtual goods, subscriptions, and advertising revenue, streamers can earn a living by entertaining and engaging their audience. Viewers are able to support their favorite streamers through direct financial contributions, channel subscriptions, and the purchase of Twitch's virtual currency, Bits. This distinctive economic ecosystem has created a viable source of income for streamers, incentivizing them to consistently produce high-quality content and engage with their viewers.

The power of live streaming in the gaming industry should not be underestimated. It offers gamers the opportunity to showcase their skills, entertain their audience, and build a dedicated fan base. The real-time aspect of streaming adds excitement and unpredictability, resonating strongly with viewers. By witnessing streamers' live reactions and emotions as they navigate challenging game levels or experience unexpected victories, viewers feel a heightened sense of camaraderie and connection.

In addition, the rise of Twitch has had profound implications for the gaming community as a whole. It has democratized the gaming industry by providing a platform for aspiring streamers to showcase their talent and gain recognition. In the past, aspiring content creators faced significant barriers to entry, including the need for expensive equipment, technical expertise, and industry connections. Twitch, with its user-friendly interface and accessibility, has leveled the playing field, allowing anyone with a passion for gaming to share their experiences and find an audience.

Twitch's impact extends beyond individual streamers. The platform has played a pivotal role in the growth of esports, providing a stage for competitive gaming tournaments to reach a global audience. Once considered a niche interest, esports has evolved into a multimillion-dollar industry, attracting mainstream attention and sponsorship deals. Twitch's live streaming capabilities have been instrumental in increasing the reach and impact of esports, contributing to its exponential growth and establishing it as a legitimate form of entertainment.

In conclusion, Twitch has revolutionized the gaming community by empowering gamers to not only play games but also share their experiences with a worldwide audience. Innovative features such as real-time interactivity and effective monetization strategies have opened up new opportunities for streamers to pursue a sustainable career in the gaming industry. Live streaming, with its ability to foster community, showcase talent, and magnify the influence of esports, has forever transformed the way we consume and engage with video games. As the Chairman and CEO of a broadcast media streaming network, I am thrilled to witness the continued evolution and impact of Twitch in shaping the future of gaming and streaming media.

YouTube: From User-Generated Content to Global Platform

Upon its launch in 2005, YouTube was predominantly viewed as a platform for sharing concise, user-generated videos. It established an avenue for individuals armed with cameras and internet access to upload and disseminate their content across the globe. However, little did we anticipate that YouTube would ultimately revolutionize both our media consumption habits and creative processes, effectively emerging as a powerful contender in relation to traditional television networks.

As the founder and CEO of a broadcast media streaming network, I have personally borne witness to this transformative progression. YouTube has indeed reshaped the media landscape, prompting the rise of a new cadre of content creators who have become veritable celebrities in their own right. What originated as a domain for cat videos and amateur vlogs has now burgeoned into an industry boasting revenue in the billions of dollars, exerting marked influence over our entertainment consumption patterns.

Crucial to YouTube's evolutionary journey is its profound impact on content creation. By virtue of accessibility and global reach, YouTube has empowered individuals to produce and disseminate content in a way previously unparalleled. The platform has democratised media production, endowing anyone harboring a creative concept and the requisite determination to produce videos and foster an audience. This has unhinged the monopoly once held by conventional gatekeepers of media, consequently lending a voice to previously unheard perspectives.

Moreover, YouTube has imparted a significant impetus to influencer marketing. With the ascent of content creators who have amassed millions of followers and subscribers, companies have become acutely aware of the power wielded by these influencers to reach and engage with their target demographics. Influencer marketing has consequently ripened into a multi-billion dollar industry, with brands fostering alliances with content creators to endorse their goods and services. YouTube has furnished influencers with a platform to cultivate their personal brands and monetize their content, endowing them with a career trajectory hitherto deemed inconceivable.

In addition to transforming content creation and influencer marketing, YouTube has substantially shaped the democratisation of media. Traditional media outlets have long governed the narrative and vetted the content destined for production and dispersal. However, YouTube has invalidated these established paradigms, affording anyone the means to publish personal content and accrue an audience, thereby puncturing the supremacy enjoyed by traditional media. This foundational shift has allowed for a broader range of perspectives and voices to permeate the public discourse, catalyzing crucial conversations.

YouTube's journey from a venue for user-generated content to a global streaming behemoth has not unfolded without challenges. The platform has faced warranted censure for its management of copyright infringement, hate speech, and inappropriate content. These issues have underscored the need for enhanced moderation and content policies to safeguard the platform's integrity as a secure and inclusive space for its users.

Notwithstanding these obstacles, it is undeniable that YouTube has fundamentally altered our media consumption habits and creative processes. It has extended avenues for individuals to share their stories and nurtured a burgeoning era of content creators. YouTube has emerged as a formidable contender within the streaming industry, posing a challenge to longstanding media conventions and illuminating a trajectory for the future of entertainment.

As an enthusiast of the social sciences, I am mesmerized by the far-reaching impact wielded by platforms such as YouTube in shaping our society and cultural milieu. Its effect on content creation, influencer marketing, and the democratisation of media ought not to be underestimated. YouTube has redefined the way we connect, entertain, and share our narratives. It has bestowed a voice upon those previously marginalized and fueled innovative and imaginative ventures. As YouTube continues to flourish and evolve, it will assuredly continue to mould the future of media and entertainment.

Disney+: The Streaming Giant's Entry Into the Market

Disney has long been synonymous with high-quality family entertainment. Over the years, they have brought joy to audiences all around the world through their animated films, theme parks, and television shows. The introduction of Disney+ reflects the company's strategic shift towards the streaming media industry, enabling them to adapt to changing consumer behaviors and maintain a competitive edge. Acknowledging the increasing popularity of on-demand video streaming, Disney took a bold step by entering this market and offering a wide range of content at an affordable price.

One of Disney's key strengths lies in its content strategy. The company boasts an impressive collection that includes not only their beloved classics, but also the extensive portfolio of franchises they have acquired over time. Disney+ provides subscribers with access to content from Disney, Pixar, Marvel, Star Wars, and National Geographic, creating a diverse and appealing selection for consumers. This vast content library gives Disney a competitive advantage, allowing them to attract a broad audience across different demographics. By offering a comprehensive platform for all their content, Disney aims to engage and retain loyal customers.

Exclusive offerings are another crucial aspect of Disney's strategy to distinguish itself in the crowded streaming market. Disney+ has introduced a range of original series, movies, and documentaries that are unique to their platform. By investing substantially in original content, they aim to differentiate themselves from competitors such as Netflix and Amazon Prime Video. For example, the immensely popular Star Wars series "The Mandalorian" became an instant hit, generating significant excitement around Disney+. This exclusive content not only draws new subscribers to the platform, but also fosters a sense of exclusivity and loyalty among existing customers.

Disney+'s entry into the streaming media market has sparked intense competition among major players in the industry. With its extensive content library and iconic brand recognition, Disney poses a significant threat to existing streaming platforms. Netflix, once the dominant force in the streaming space, now faces the challenge of retaining subscribers in the face of increasing competition. In response, Netflix has made substantial investments in original programming, creating content that appeals to a diverse range of audiences. Amazon Prime Video has also made notable progress in the streaming market, leveraging its e-commerce platform and global distribution network to reach a wide-ranging international audience.

While the competition among streaming platforms is intense, it is ultimately the consumers who reap the benefits of this rivalry. With more options available, consumers can now choose platforms that align with their specific preferences and interests. This competition is driving innovation, resulting in improved user experiences and a greater variety of content offerings. Streaming platforms are investing in advanced algorithms and personalized recommendations to enhance the user experience and ensure that subscribers have access to the content they love.

Disney's entry into the streaming media market has unquestionably disrupted the industry. By leveraging their strong brand, extensive content library, and exclusive offerings, Disney+ has rapidly established itself as a major player in the streaming landscape. The success of Disney+ has compelled other streaming platforms to reassess their strategies and make significant investments in content creation and customer retention. As the streaming market continues to evolve, it will be fascinating to observe how Disney+ and other platforms adapt to changing consumer behaviors, technological advancements, and emerging market trends.

In conclusion, Disney+ has made a formidable foray into the streaming media market. With its vast content library, exclusive offerings, and strong brand recognition, it has disrupted the industry and posed a significant challenge to existing streaming platforms. By recognizing the importance of content strategy, investing in original programming, and fostering healthy competition, Disney+ has carved out a unique position for itself in the rapidly evolving streaming landscape. As the battle for streaming supremacy persists, it is evident that Disney's entry has forever transformed the way we consume and enjoy entertainment.

Independent Success Stories and Niche Streaming Platforms

To comprehend the significance of these success stories, it is imperative to initially acknowledge the challenges faced by independent and niche streaming platforms. Amidst the prevalence of major streaming platforms such as Netflix, Amazon Prime Video, and Hulu, it can appear daunting to venture into the market as a small player. However, these success stories illustrate that there is still scope for innovation and targeted content delivery.

One such success story is the platform "IndieFlix." Helmed by filmmakers Scilla Andreen and Carlo Scandiuzzi, IndieFlix is committed to showcasing independent films and documentaries. While major streaming platforms may possess an extensive content library, IndieFlix recognizes the requirement for a platform that caters specifically to independent creators and prides itself on presenting a curated collection that prioritizes quality over quantity.

IndieFlix's unique value proposition lies in its commitment to supporting independent filmmakers and providing a distribution platform that bridges their work with a global audience. Through this initiative, they have fostered a community of impassioned artists and film enthusiasts, cultivating an environment that fosters creativity and offers recognition to lesser-known talents.

Another noteworthy success story is the niche streaming platform "Gaiam TV." Specializing in wellness, spirituality, and personal growth content, Gaiam TV has positioned itself as a sanctuary for individuals seeking a mindful and holistic approach to their lives. With an inventory comprising instructional videos, documentaries, and original programming, Gaiam TV has established itself in an industry where mainstream platforms often overlook such niche content.

Gaiam TV's target audience is comprised of individuals who prioritize their physical and mental well-being, seeking inspiration, guidance, and knowledge to lead a balanced life. By collaborating with renowned experts, spiritual leaders, and practitioners, Gaiam TV offers a diverse range of content that supports personal growth, meditation, yoga, and holistic healing. Their platform has fostered a community where individuals can congregate, learn, and connect with like-minded individuals who share their passions and aspirations.

Delving into another niche, we encounter "Shudder," a streaming platform exclusively devoted to horror content. While horror films have long enjoyed a loyal following, Shudder saw untapped potential in creating a platform solely for horror enthusiasts. By selecting a collection of classic horror movies, contemporary thrillers, and original programming, Shudder carved out its own niche, catering to adrenaline junkies craving spine-chilling experiences.

What sets Shudder apart is its immersive and interactive approach to content delivery. Recognizing that horror fans revel in engaging and discussing their preferred genre, Shudder provides a platform for community interaction, permitting users to share their thoughts, recommendations, and even participate in live events. This innovative approach has fostered a sense of belonging and excitement within the horror community, solidifying Shudder as a leading platform in its niche.

Beyond these specific success stories, independent filmmakers and content creators have also discovered avenues for success through platforms such as YouTube and Vimeo. Although these platforms may not fit the niche category of the aforementioned examples, they serve as powerful instruments for independent content creators to reach a global audience.

Particularly, YouTube has been the birthplace of numerous success stories, where individuals began with nothing more than a camera, passion, and a distinctive talent or perspective. From makeup tutorials to comedic sketches, YouTube has empowered individuals to become their own directors, producers, and stars, generating content that resonates with millions worldwide.

Similarly, Vimeo has established itself as a go-to platform for independent filmmakers. It offers a space to showcase their work, connect with fellow creators, and garner recognition within the film industry. By providing a platform that upholds high-quality content and artistic integrity, Vimeo has become a launching pad for many independent filmmakers, enabling them to secure funding, distribution deals, and even accolades at prestigious international film festivals.

These independent success stories and niche streaming platforms are a testament to the power of carving out a unique space in a competitive industry. They demonstrate that passion, innovation, and an in-depth comprehension of specific audiences can immensely contribute to achieving success in the constantly evolving realm of streaming media.

By emphasizing their unique value propositions, target audiences, and innovative approaches to content delivery, this subchapter aims to inspire aspiring content creators, filmmakers, and entrepreneurs. It exemplifies that even in an industry dominated by major players, there is still an opportunity for underdogs to leave their mark and prosper. With a suitable blend of creativity, dedication, and a genuine connection with specific audiences, independent success stories will persist in shaping and redefining the landscape of streaming media.

Chapter 16: Social Impact of Streaming Media

Streaming for Social Change

The strength of streaming lies in its capacity to engage and mesmerize audiences. With a simple click, individuals with internet access can conveniently access a vast array of audio and video content that covers a wide spectrum of social issues. Streaming platforms have effectively democratized information availability, enabling people to educate themselves about the world and take action.

Firstly, let us delve into how streaming media has successfully raised awareness about social issues. In an era where traditional media often prioritizes sensationalized stories or neglects important topics, streaming platforms have allowed passionate individuals and organizations to amplify their voices and shed light on otherwise overlooked issues. For instance, Netflix has become prominent for its social issue documentaries, such as "13th" which exposes the harsh realities of the American prison system, and "The Social Dilemma" which investigates the impact of social media on society. These films have sparked conversations, ignited activism, and prompted viewers to reassess their own beliefs and attitudes.

Furthermore, streaming has been employed as a tool for virtual protest. Recent years have showcased the power of streaming platforms to mobilize large-scale movements and provide a voice to marginalized communities. A notable example is the global Women's March in 2017. While millions physically demonstrated for gender equality, streaming platforms ensured that those unable to participate in person could still engage virtually. Broadcasting live on platforms like Facebook, YouTube, and Periscope, people worldwide were able to witness the magnitude of the movement and join the conversation, fostering a sense of unity and solidarity.

Streaming media has also facilitated conversations leading to meaningful societal impact. Podcasts, for example, have become a popular medium for in-depth discussions on a range of topics. By providing a platform for experts, activists, and everyday individuals to share their insights and experiences, podcasts have become catalysts for change. Shows like "Pod Save the People," hosted by renowned activist DeRay Mckesson, delve into pressing social issues and provide actionable steps for listeners to contribute to creating change. These conversations not only inform and educate but also empower individuals to actively participate in shaping a more just and equitable society.

To further illustrate the potential of streaming media for social change, let us examine a few notable research studies. A study conducted by Leeds Beckett University, for instance, found that streaming platforms effectively raised awareness and stimulated discussions about mental health. By featuring personal stories, expert interviews, and support resources, streaming platforms created an accessible and safe environment for individuals to learn about mental health issues and seek assistance when necessary.

Another study conducted by the University of Oxford focused on the impact of live streaming protests on social media platforms. The findings demonstrated that live streams not only increased the overall reach and visibility of protests but also facilitated the organization and coordination of collective action. The real-time nature of live streaming allowed activists to reach audiences beyond their physical location, resulting in a broader impact and increased participation.

As streaming media continues to evolve, its potential for social change also expands. In addition to raising awareness, organizing protests, and fostering conversations, streaming platforms have the ability to drive fundraising efforts for social causes. Many nonprofit organizations have embraced live streaming for virtual fundraising events, enabling supporters from various locations to contribute and make a difference.

It is crucial to acknowledge that streaming media for social change does face challenges. Despite the undeniable increase in access to diverse perspectives due to the democratization of information, there has also been a surge in echo chambers and the dissemination of misinformation. Users must critically evaluate the content they consume and engage in constructive discussions that promote understanding and empathy.

In conclusion, streaming platforms have emerged as powerful instruments for social change, providing a medium for raising awareness, organizing protests, and fostering meaningful conversations. From documentaries that expose societal injustices to live streams of protests transcending geographical boundaries, streaming media possesses the potential to create a more informed and engaged citizenry. As we navigate the digital landscape, it is vital to responsibly harness the power of streaming media, empowering individuals to become informed advocates and agents of change in their communities and beyond.

Empowering Marginalized Communities Through Streaming

When examining the ways in which streaming has empowered marginalized communities, it is essential to acknowledge the historical context that has resulted in their marginalization. Discrimination, bias, and systemic barriers have long suppressed the narratives of minority groups, making it challenging for them to overcome the traditional media gatekeepers. This lack of representation has perpetuated stereotypes, restricted opportunities, and excluded these communities from shaping the narratives that define their lives.

However, streaming platforms have emerged as a democratizing force, offering an accessible and cost-effective means of sharing stories and knowledge. By no longer relying on traditional media channels, underrepresented individuals and communities have embraced streaming as a tool for self-expression and empowerment. These platforms have provided marginalized voices the opportunity to reclaim their narratives, celebrate their culture, and foster understanding among diverse communities.

One way in which streaming has empowered marginalized communities is through the provision of a space for the creation and distribution of alternative media. Independent filmmakers, artists, journalists, and content creators from underrepresented backgrounds now have a platform to showcase their work without being subjected to the gatekeeping mechanisms of traditional media. In doing so, they can challenge prevailing narratives and offer perspectives that have long been overlooked or disregarded.

For instance, the rise of video-sharing platforms such as YouTube and Vimeo has paved the way for a new generation of diverse content creators who address topics ranging from social justice issues to the preservation of cultural heritage. These creators have harnessed the power of streaming to reach a global audience, amplifying their voices and making a significant impact on society. By sharing their experiences and viewpoints, they confront stereotypes and provide nuanced understandings of complex issues.

Streaming platforms have also facilitated easier connections between marginalized communities that share similar experiences and challenges. Online communities and forums centered around specific interests or identities have thrived, enabling individuals to find support, exchange resources, and collaborate on initiatives that address their unique needs. These virtual spaces foster a sense of belonging and solidarity, empowering individuals by reminding them that they are not alone in their struggles.

Moreover, streaming has provided marginalized communities with the ability to curate their narratives and redefine how they are represented in mainstream media. For far too long, the media has perpetuated harmful stereotypes and misrepresented marginalized groups. By assuming control of their storytelling, these communities can now offer genuine portrayals of their culture, history, and lived experiences, challenging the dominant narratives of mainstream media.

Documentary filmmakers, in particular, have embraced streaming as a powerful tool to highlight critical social issues and uplift marginalized voices. Through thought-provoking narratives, these documentaries shed light on the systemic injustices faced by marginalized communities, and facilitate discussions that lead to social change. Streaming platforms offer a global distribution network, enabling these films to reach audiences beyond the traditional documentary film festival circuit.

For example, the documentary "13th," directed by Ava DuVernay, explores the legacy of racial inequality in the United States criminal justice system. By making this documentary available on streaming platforms like Netflix, DuVernay ensured that the film reached a wide audience, resulting in increased awareness and sparked conversations about racial injustice. Streaming has democratized access to these stories, prompting meaningful discussions and fostering social change.

Streaming has also demonstrated its effectiveness as a tool for education and empowerment within marginalized communities. Through the availability of online courses, workshops, and webinars, individuals who may not have had access to traditional educational opportunities can now expand their knowledge and skills. Streaming platforms have democratized education, making it accessible to individuals who face financial, geographic, or cultural barriers. Offering courses on various subjects, these platforms have empowered individuals to acquire new skills, pursue their passions, and advance their careers.

Additionally, streaming has allowed marginalized communities to document and preserve their cultural heritage. By sharing traditional practices, customs, and art forms through live broadcasts or recorded videos, these communities can now safeguard their heritage and prevent its loss or oblivion. This has led to a greater appreciation and understanding of diverse cultural expressions, contributing to a more inclusive and interconnected global society.

In conclusion, streaming media has played a significant role in empowering marginalized communities. By providing a platform for underrepresented voices to be heard, streaming platforms have challenged stereotypes, promoted inclusivity, and contributed to social change. These platforms have democratized access to storytelling, education, and cultural heritage preservation, enabling marginalized communities to reclaim their narratives. As streaming continues to evolve, it is imperative that we recognize and support the power it holds in amplifying voices, fostering understanding, and promoting a more equitable society.

Building Virtual Communities Through Streaming

As an esteemed social science researcher and the Chief Executive Officer of a prominent broadcast media streaming network, I have had the privilege of observing firsthand the transformative influence of streaming media in constructing virtual communities. Within this subchapter, we shall delve into the profound role that streaming platforms play in uniting likeminded individuals, fostering a sense of belonging, and nurturing collective identity in the digital era.

The emergence of streaming technology has completely revolutionized the manner in which individuals consume audio and video content. With a mere click of a button, people from all walks of life can now access an expansive range of content that aligns with their interests, passions, and values. Streaming platforms have effectively bridged the formerly insurmountable geographical gaps that kept individuals apart, providing them the means to connect and establish virtual communities with a mere internet connection and a shared interest.

One of the most remarkable aspects of streaming media lies in its ability to forge connections based on shared interests. Whether it be a fervor for culinary arts, an ardent love for independent music, or a profound fascination with astrophysics, streaming communities tailored to almost every conceivable niche interest exist. These communities act as virtual gathering spaces, drawing individuals who share analogous passions and enabling them to connect, learn from one another, and nurture enduring relationships.

Notably, what sets streaming communities apart from other online spaces is the sense of belonging they nurture. On traditional social media platforms, individuals are often inundated with information and advertisements which detrimentally impacts their capacity to cultivate meaningful connections. Streaming communities, in contrast, provide a more focused and engrossing experience. Through the curation of content and the offering of specialized features, streaming platforms create spaces wherein participants can genuinely engage with their passions and connect with others who share those same interests.

Digital streaming communities bestow a refreshing respite from the cacophony and disarray that plagues numerous social media platforms. These communities furnish individuals with a space wherein they can delve deeply into their interests, explore novel ideas, and partake in thoughtful discussions. Such immersive experiences enable individuals to foster genuine connections with others who not only share their interests but also comprehend the nuances and intricacies of their passions.

Additionally, streaming platforms possess the advantage of facilitating real-time interactions, thus further enhancing the sense of community and belonging. Through live streaming, viewers can actively engage with both content creators and fellow community members, participating in discussions, posing inquiries, and offering insightful perspectives.

This immediacy engenders a dynamic environment wherein individuals feel acknowledged, esteemed, and comprehended.

Furthermore, streaming communities play a pivotal role in shaping collective identity. In the digital era, individuals are increasingly defined by their online associations and the communities to which they belong. Streaming platforms provide individuals with a platform to express their identities and find validation within their shared interests and values. For instance, a streaming community devoted to environmental conservation enables members not only to deliberate upon environmental issues but also empowers them to effect collective change and materialize a tangible impact in the world.

It is noteworthy to recognize that the establishment of virtual communities through streaming is not restricted to the realm of entertainment or leisurely pursuits. Nonprofit organizations and social impact initiatives have enthusiastically embraced streaming media as a potent instrument for community building and advocacy. By leveraging the extensive range and engagement fostered by streaming platforms, these organizations can connect with supporters, educate the public, and rally individuals around a common cause. Streaming has become a catalyst for social transformation, amplifying voices and facilitating collective action on a global scale.

In conclusion, streaming media has unequivocally revolutionized the manner in which we connect, share, and construct communities in the digital era. Streaming platforms offer virtual spaces wherein like-minded individuals can congregate, nurturing a sense of belonging and collective identity. Through the curation of content, the facilitation of real-time interactions, and the empowerment of individuals to express their passions, streaming communities provide immersive and meaningful experiences that transcend mere entertainment. As the streaming industry continues to flourish and evolve, so too will the opportunities to construct virtual communities that unite people, inspire transformation, and shape our collective future.

Chapter 17: Ethical Considerations in Streaming Media

Privacy and Data Security in Streaming

It is of utmost importance to establish a precise comprehension of the terms "privacy" and "data security" in the realm of streaming media. In this particular context, privacy refers to an individual's right to control and safeguard their personal information from unauthorized access, usage, or distribution without their explicit consent. Conversely, data security pertains to the methodologies and measures- henceforth referred to as safeguards - employed to protect the confidentiality, integrity, and availability of data.

Streaming platforms, whether for audio or video content, have drastically altered the manner in which we consume media. As digital platforms proliferate, data has evidently become the principal fuel that powers the streaming industry. Whenever a user engages with a streaming service, an extensive cache of data is generated, encompassing viewing habits, preferences, and personal details such as names, email addresses, and device identifiers. The collection of this user data is vital for companies in tailoring their offerings, ameliorating their services, and effectively targeting advertisements.

However, the copious collection and utilization of user data within the streaming ecosystem give rise to genuine privacy concerns. Users may feel discomposed by the realization that their personal information is being harvested without their explicit consent. The obscure nature of data collection and usage, unaccompanied by proper transparency, can engender a breach of trust between streaming service providers and their users.

To address these concerns and safeguard user privacy, it is imperious that data protection measures be implemented. Encryption represents an exemplar measure that ensures data transmitted between devices and streaming servers remains secure and impervious to unauthorized entities. Secure sockets layer (SSL) encryption is an illustrative example of a means to encrypt data sent over the internet, rendering it formidable for hackers to intercept or decipher.

Furthermore, streaming platforms should adopt stringent access control mechanisms and authentication protocols to prohibit unauthorized parties from gaining access to user data. Employing robust passwords, two-factor authentication, and confining access privileges exclusively to individuals who necessitate the data can significantly diminish the risk of data breaches.

Additionally, the industry must embrace data minimization practices, wherein solely essential data requisite for the provision of services is collected and retained. This approach confines the exposure of sensitive user information and diminishes the potential repercussion in the event of a data breach.

It is unequivocal that ethical considerations concerning data privacy in the streaming ecosystem must not be disregarded. Companies must adhere to ethical standards in the collection, storage, and usage of user data. Transparency should be the bedrock of their practices, ensuring that users are well-informed about the types of data being collected, its intended usage, and the entities with whom it may be shared. This serves to empower users to make comprehensively informed decisions and fosters a climate of trust between service providers and their audience.

Furthermore, companies must secure explicit consent from users before collecting and utilizing their data. This necessitates clear, unambiguous language that comprehensively elucidates the purpose and scope of data collection. Users should be afforded the opportunity to opt out or restrict the usage of their personal information, thus enabling them to effectively retain a certain level of jurisdiction over their data.

In conjunction with these ethical considerations, it is indispensable to recognize the potential biases and discrimination that may ensue from the employment of user data. Streaming platforms often rely on algorithms to proffer content suggestions based on user preferences and viewing history. While this approach may enhance the user experience, it also harbors the potential to cement existing biases or engender filter bubbles that limit exposure to diverse perspectives. Consequently, it is paramount for companies to periodically assess and rectify these biases with the aim of promoting impartiality and inclusivity within the streaming ecosystem.

As the streaming media industry perpetuates its growth and evolution, privacy and data security will continue to occupy the vanguard. It is incumbent upon service providers to prioritize the safeguarding of user data, adhere to ethical practices, and cultivate an environment typified by trust and transparency. By doing so, they can not only amend user experiences but also perpetuate a more secure and reliable streaming ecosystem.

Content Moderation and Responsible Streaming

Content moderation in the streaming media industry is a highly complex task that requires meticulous consideration of various factors. Streaming platforms bear the responsibility of determining the appropriateness of user-generated content within their systems. Striking a delicate balance between ensuring freedom of expression and safeguarding users against harmful or inappropriate content poses a significant challenge.

One of the most pressing issues in content moderation is the prevalence of hate speech online. Streaming platforms serve as platforms for individuals with diverse backgrounds and ideologies to express themselves, making it indispensable to take measures against hate speech. Research has demonstrated that exposure to hate speech can result in psychological harm, foster a toxic online environment, and perpetuate discrimination and prejudice. Streaming platforms must actively monitor and promptly remove any hate speech that infringes upon their community guidelines and terms of service.

In addition to hate speech, the dissemination of misinformation has become a significant concern in the streaming media industry. In the era of social media and online platforms, misinformation can rapidly spread and have real-life consequences. Streaming platforms must implement strategies to detect and combat misinformation as it poses a threat to democratic processes, public health, and public safety. Research has revealed that streaming platforms' algorithms can inadvertently amplify misinformation, leading to its swift propagation. Consequently, it is of utmost importance for platforms to develop robust systems for fact-checking and validating user-generated content.

Another challenge in content moderation within the streaming media industry entails addressing harmful or graphic content shared online. While upholding freedom of expression is crucial, platforms must also shield users from exposure to violent, explicit, or distressing material. Research has indicated that exposure to such content can have detrimental psychological effects, particularly on vulnerable populations such as children and individuals with mental health conditions. Streaming platforms must swiftly and efficiently implement measures to identify and remove such content, thereby safeguarding the well-being of their users.

Maintaining a delicate balance between content moderation responsibilities and the principles of freedom of expression is a complex task. Streaming platforms should establish clear guidelines and policies outlining acceptable and unacceptable content types. These guidelines must be effectively conveyed to users and consistently enforced. However, it is vital to strike a balance that encourages diverse perspectives and promotes responsible streaming practices. Platforms should equip users with tools and resources to report content that they believe infringes on community guidelines, all while offering guidance on responsible content creation and consumption.

Effectively addressing the challenges of content moderation in the streaming media industry necessitates collaboration and engagement with stakeholders. Streaming platforms can collaborate closely with governments, regulatory bodies, civil society organizations, and academic institutions to establish best practices and guidelines for responsible content moderation. Such collaboratives efforts can ensure that content moderation policies are grounded in evidence-based research and conform to legal and ethical considerations.

Investing in technology and human resources is also vital for streaming platforms to enhance content moderation endeavors. Artificial intelligence and machine learning algorithms can significantly contribute to automating the content detection and removal process. Nevertheless, it is essential to acknowledge the limitations of technology and the indispensable need for human intervention in making nuanced decisions. Platforms should employ a combination of automated systems and human moderators to ensure precise and appropriate content moderation.

In conclusion, content moderation plays a pivotal role in responsible streaming within the media industry. Streaming platforms bear the responsibility of monitoring and moderating user-generated content, addressing issues such as hate speech, misinformation, and harmful content. Achieving a balance between freedom of expression and user protection necessitates careful consideration and collaboration with stakeholders. By implementing robust content moderation strategies, investing in technology and human resources, and fostering responsible streaming practices, platforms can engender a safer and more inclusive streaming environment for all users.

Mental Health and Well-being in the Streaming Era

As a researcher in the field of social science, I have always been intrigued by the impact of media consumption on our mental well-being. With the emergence of streaming services and the growing amount of time individuals spend engaging in online audio and video content, it is imperative to comprehend the potential effects on our psychological health.

Research findings have indicated that excessive streaming can have adverse consequences on our mental well-being. Prolonged exposure to screens can result in feelings of isolation, anxiety, and even depression. Immersing ourselves for long hours in fictional realms or indulging in extensive binge-watching sessions can detach us from our real lives and relationships. Therefore, it is crucial to acknowledge the emotional toll this behavior can take and take proactive measures to establish a healthy equilibrium.

On the flip side, streaming media can also have positive effects on our mental health. It serves as a source of amusement, relaxation, and an escape from the daily realities of life. Connecting with characters and storylines can provide a sense of belonging and emotional support, particularly for individuals who experience isolation or loneliness. It can be a valuable tool for self-care and a means to alleviate stress.

Nevertheless, as is the case with most things in life, maintaining balance is imperative. In order to enjoy the benefits of streaming media without compromising our mental well-being, it is important to adopt strategies that foster a healthy streaming routine.

Primarily, it is crucial that we remain mindful of our streaming habits and evaluate whether they impede other areas of our lives. Are we neglecting significant relationships, responsibilities, or self-care activities due to excessive streaming? If so, it may be necessary to reassess our priorities and set boundaries around our media consumption.

One practical approach is to establish designated times for streaming and adhere to them. By establishing a structured approach to consuming entertainment, we mitigate the risk of indulging excessively and thoughtlessly. This allows us to savor our preferred shows and movies while still being mindful of our other commitments.

Additionally, diversifying our media consumption is a worthwhile strategy. Instead of solely relying on streaming services, we can explore alternative forms of entertainment, such as reading books or participating in physical activities. This not only diminishes our screen time but also cultivates a more balanced approach to leisure activities.

Expanding upon the concept of balance, engaging in digital well-being practices is crucial. These practices encompass adopting a mindful approach to our overall technology usage and implementing strategies to mitigate the negative consequences of excessive screen time. One practical way to promote digital well-being is to designate times or areas where screens are prohibited. This fosters a healthier relationship with technology and affords us the opportunity to reconnect with our surroundings and ourselves.

Furthermore, being discerning in the content we consume is essential. The streaming era provides an extensive range of options, yet not all content is equal in terms of mental health and overall well-being. It is important to remain mindful of the themes, messages, and emotional impact of the shows and movies we choose to view. Opting for content that aligns with our values and promotes positive emotions can contribute to a healthier media diet.

Lastly, it is vital to recognize that streaming media constitutes just one facet of our lives. While it can provide entertainment and pleasure, it should not commandeer our existence entirely. It is imperative that we nurture other aspects of our lives, such as relationships, hobbies, and personal growth. By diversifying our experiences and interests, we can establish a more well-rounded and gratifying life.

In conclusion, the advent of the streaming era has unquestionably revolutionized our consumption of audio and video content. While it offers numerous advantages, it is vital to acknowledge the potential risks to our mental health and well-being. By adopting strategies to maintain a healthy streaming routine, promoting digital well-being, and remaining mindful of the content we consume, we can navigate the streaming era in a manner that enriches our lives rather than detracts from them. Remember, it is all about achieving the right balance and making conscious choices within the vast sea of streaming options.

Chapter 18: Streaming Media and Education

E-Learning Platforms and MOOCs

Online learning has experienced a significant surge in popularity in recent years for a variety of compelling reasons. The advantages it brings are wide-ranging and hold the potential to profoundly transform traditional education systems. One of the principal benefits of e-learning platforms is their accessibility. These platforms provide a democratized space where individuals, regardless of their location, can access high-quality educational resources. Whether residing in a remote village or working professionals aiming to enhance their skills, e-learning platforms offer flexibility and convenience often lacking in traditional education.

The democratization of knowledge is yet another noteworthy aspect of streaming platforms. In the past, access to education was restricted to those who possessed the financial means or who lived in close proximity to educational institutions. E-learning platforms have dismantled these barriers and made education accessible to a global audience. This democratization ensures that individuals from diverse socio-economic backgrounds and geographical locations can expand their education and skills, thereby unlocking greater economic and social opportunities.

Additionally, streaming platforms have played a crucial role in advancing inclusive education. Through features like closed captioning and compatibility with assistive technologies, these platforms accommodate individuals with disabilities or special learning needs. This inclusivity ensures that no one is left behind in their pursuit of education.

However, it is crucial to acknowledge the challenges inherent to online education. One primary concern revolves around maintaining student engagement in a virtual learning environment. Without the immediate feedback and interaction provided in traditional classrooms, students may encounter difficulties staying motivated and actively participating in their courses. As an e-learning practitioner and educator, I have grappled with this challenge and have learned that designing interactive and stimulating learning experiences is pivotal for maintaining student engagement. Integration of multimedia elements, such as videos, quizzes, discussion forums, and virtual collaboration tools, can significantly contribute to fostering a rich and meaningful online learning experience.

Another challenge of online education lies in ensuring the quality of learning outcomes. With the proliferation of e-learning platforms and massive open online courses (MOOCs), the market is saturated with courses of varying quality. It is imperative for educational institutions, content creators, and platforms themselves to employ robust quality assurance mechanisms. This entails rigorous course design, pedagogical approaches that foster active learning, and continuous assessment and feedback to ensure students are attaining their learning goals.

Furthermore, there exists a risk of creating a digital divide where individuals without internet access or technological resources are excluded from reaping the benefits of online education. Addressing this divide mandates concerted efforts from governments, non-profit organizations, and private entities to offer affordable internet access and equip underserved communities with the requisite technological infrastructure. Only by tackling these systemic disparities can we truly unlock the potential of e-learning platforms and MOOCs in democratizing education.

Research studies have evidenced the positive impact of e-learning platforms and MOOCs on student learning outcomes. A study conducted by researchers from Harvard and MIT set out to examine the effectiveness of edX, one of the largest MOOC platforms. The study revealed that students who completed online courses fared better in assessments compared to those who dropped out. This finding suggests that, when effectively utilized, streaming platforms have the capacity to facilitate enriching learning experiences and yield positive educational outcomes.

Another research study carried out by researchers from Stanford University explored the accessibility of online courses. The study unveiled that online learners hail from diverse backgrounds and possess varying motivations for enrolling in courses. This diversity lends value to the learning experience by fostering cross-cultural understanding and cultivating a global community of learners. E-learning platforms not only offer learning opportunities but also serve as a platform for collaboration and knowledge exchange among individuals from diverse backgrounds.

In conclusion, e-learning platforms and MOOCs represent potent tools that have revolutionized the field of streaming media and educational systems at a global scale. The benefits they offer, such as accessibility, democratization of knowledge, and inclusive education, render them indispensable in the modern world. However, challenges, such as maintaining student engagement and ensuring the attainment of quality learning outcomes, must be addressed to realize the full potential of online education. Through the combined efforts of educators, policymakers, and technology providers, we can forge a future where education is genuinely accessible to all, irrespective of their circumstances.

Educational Content Creation and Curation

In the current era of digital advancements, the field of education has undergone a significant metamorphosis. Conventional teaching and learning methods have been supplemented by the power of streaming media, enabling educators to reach a wider audience and offer innovative learning experiences. As a researcher in the social sciences, a social entrepreneur, and a documentary filmmaker, I have personally witnessed the profound influence of streaming media on the creation and curation of educational content.

Streaming platforms present a distinct opportunity for educators to generate and disseminate educational content. With the proliferation of platforms such as YouTube, Vimeo, and Twitch, anyone with internet access can assume the role of an educator and share their expertise with the global community. This democratization of education has opened new avenues for content creation, fostering the exchange of diverse perspectives and ideas.

The process of educational content creation commences with the identification of specific learning objectives. Whether the aim is to teach a foreign language, elucidate complex mathematical concepts, or offer professional development opportunities, educators must possess a clear understanding of their intended outcomes for the content. This clarity of purpose guides the entire content creation process, ensuring that the resultant material is focused and impactful.

Once the learning objective is established, educators can commence the development process for their content. This may involve various techniques, such as scripted videos, live demonstrations, interactive quizzes, or augmented reality experiences. The selection of a format hinges upon the nature of the subject matter and the target audience. For instance, a chemistry experiment may be better suited for a live demonstration, whereas a history lesson may be more effectively conveyed through a scripted video.

Quality assurance stands as a vital aspect of educational content creation. As educators, we bear the responsibility of ensuring the accuracy, thorough research, and engaging nature of the information we provide. This entails conducting exhaustive research, consulting subject matter experts, and fact-checking our content. By adhering to these standards, we can establish credibility and trust among our audience, cultivating an enriching learning environment.

Collaboration emerges as another noteworthy element in educational content creation. Thanks to the advent of streaming platforms, educators are no longer confined to their individual expertise. They can collaborate with fellow educators, experts, and professionals to create comprehensive and interdisciplinary learning experiences. By pooling resources and sharing knowledge, educators can produce content enriched with diverse perspectives and insights.

Curation plays a significant role in the development of educational content. As the Chairman and CEO of a broadcast media streaming network, I have personally witnessed the importance of curating high-quality educational content. Curators must meticulously select and organize content that aligns with learning objectives, thus offering learners a curated path towards knowledge acquisition. This process entails evaluating the credibility and relevance of available content, ensuring that it meets specific educational standards.

The process of curation further involves the sequencing and organization of content in a logical and coherent manner. This empowers learners to progress systematically through a content library, building on their existing knowledge and skills. Curators must also consider the diversity of learners and cater to different learning styles, ensuring that their content is accessible and engaging for all.

As educational content creators and curators, we must continuously adapt and evolve to meet the ever-changing needs and preferences of our audience. This necessitates staying updated on technological advancements and integrating new tools and techniques into our content creation process. For instance, the incorporation of virtual reality or gamification elements can enhance the learning experience and make it more immersive and engaging.

In conclusion, educational content creation and curation are integral components of streaming media. Educators and content creators possess the opportunity to leverage streaming platforms to develop and disseminate educational content on a global scale. Through meticulous planning, collaboration, and quality assurance, educational content can be crafted to meet specific learning objectives while retaining credibility and relevance. Curation plays a pivotal role in organizing this content in a meaningful manner, enabling learners to navigate a curated path of knowledge acquisition. With ongoing technological advancements, the field of educational content creation and curation is poised to expand and evolve, offering even greater opportunities for educators to leave a lasting impact in the digital learning landscape.

The Future of Streaming Media in Education

As a researcher in the field of social sciences, a social entrepreneur, a documentary filmmaker, a nonprofit executive, and the Chairman and CEO of a broadcast media streaming network, my interest has always been drawn to the ways in which technology can enhance and revolutionize the educational landscape. Streaming media has already made a significant impact on education, granting students and teachers access to an extensive range of information and resources. However, as technology continues to advance, it is becoming increasingly evident that streaming media has the potential to play an even more substantial role in education.

One of the most exhilarating developments in this realm is the emergence of virtual reality (VR) and augmented reality (AR) technologies. Although VR has primarily been associated with gaming and entertainment, its impact on education cannot be disregarded. Just imagine a biology student having the opportunity to virtually dissect a frog or a history student exploring ancient civilizations through an authentic virtual tour. With the integration of VR, rather than merely reading textbooks or watching videos, students can fully immerse themselves in the subject matter, engaging all their senses and fostering a profound understanding.

Similarly, augmented reality (AR) offers educators an array of new possibilities to enhance the learning experience. Through AR, students can superimpose digital information onto the physical world, bringing static images and objects to life. For instance, a chemistry student could utilize an AR application to visualize the molecular structure of a compound, or an art student could use AR to observe a painting come to life with animated elements. AR has the potential to make abstract concepts more tangible and interactive, consequently allowing for an immersive and dynamic learning experience.

Certainly, the adoption of VR and AR in education necessitates substantial investments in both hardware and software. Educational institutions must ensure they possess the necessary infrastructure to support these technologies, such as high-speed internet connections and VR/AR-enabled devices. However, as the cost of these technologies continues to decrease, their accessibility in the educational realm is undeniably destined to increase.

In addition to exploring these emerging technologies, it is crucial to address the importance of digital literacy within the context of streaming media in education. Just as students learn how to read and write, they must also learn how to navigate and critically evaluate digital media. This includes comprehending concepts such as online privacy, digital citizenship, and information literacy. As streaming media becomes an integral part of the educational experience, students must develop the essential skills to engage with and make sense of the information they encounter.

Equitable access to streaming media is another significant consideration. While streaming media has the potential to equalize educational opportunities by providing access to resources and information irrespective of geographic location, income level, or physical ability, it is vital to ensure that all students have equal access to these tools and resources. This demands addressing the "digital divide" or the disparity in access to technology and internet connectivity among different populations. Schools and policymakers must collaborate to bridge this gap and provide equitable access to streaming media for all students.

Furthermore, we must consider the role of streaming media in lifelong learning and professional development. As technology advances and industries evolve, workers will increasingly need to acquire new skills and knowledge throughout their careers. Streaming media can serve as a valuable tool for delivering training and educational content to professionals in a convenient and flexible manner. Whether it be through online courses, webinars, or virtual conferences, streaming media can aid individuals in staying current and adapting to the changing demands of the workforce.

The future of streaming media in education is both exciting and brimming with possibilities. From virtual reality and augmented reality to digital literacy and equitable access, several factors will shape the manner in which streaming media is utilized within educational settings. As educators, it is our responsibility to embrace these technologies, foster digital literacy among our students, and work towards creating a more inclusive and accessible educational experience for all. By harnessing the power of streaming media, we have the ability to revolutionize education and empower students with the necessary tools to thrive in the digital age.

In conclusion, as I wrap up this subchapter, I am eagerly anticipating the continued impact of streaming media on the future of education. Drawing from my extensive research and experience, I can confidently assert that the possibilities are endless. It is up to us, as educators, to wholeheartedly embrace these technologies, adapt our teaching methods accordingly, and provide our students with the most exceptional educational experiences possible. Only by doing so can we fully unleash the potential of streaming media in education and prepare future generations for the digital world that awaits them.

19

Chapter 19: Streaming Media in Sports

Over-the-Top (OTT) Sports Streaming

In the past ten years, there has been a notable shift in media consumption as a result of the rise of streaming technology. Streaming has transformed the way we engage with movies, music, news, and even sports events. As expected, sports broadcasting has also embraced this disruptive trend, with the emergence of over-the-top (OTT) sports streaming services. These services have become a formidable presence, providing sports fans with direct access to live events from the convenience of their own homes or any location with an internet connection.

As the Chairman and CEO of a broadcast media streaming network, I have personally witnessed the profound impact of OTT sports streaming on the industry. It has not only revolutionized the way sports content is consumed but has also created new opportunities for broadcasters, advertisers, and fans alike.

One of the key advantages of OTT sports streaming is the increased accessibility it offers to fans. Gone are the days when sports enthusiasts had to rely solely on traditional broadcasting networks to watch their favorite games. Platforms like Netflix, Hulu, and Amazon Prime Video have accustomed consumers to unlimited content at their fingertips, and OTT sports streaming services have tapped into this demand for convenience. These services make it possible for fans to access live games on a wide range of devices, including smartphones, tablets, and smart TVs.

This enhanced accessibility has not only expanded the audience of sports events but has also given fans more control over their viewing experiences. Previously, viewers had to conform to broadcasting schedules and plan their routines around games. OTT sports streaming services have changed this dynamic by allowing fans to watch games at their own convenience. Whether it's pausing a live match for a snack break or rewinding to catch a remarkable goal, viewers now have the ability to create personalized and interactive experiences.

Moreover, OTT sports streaming services have broken down geographical barriers, leading to a new level of global fan engagement. Access to live sports events was traditionally limited by geographical boundaries, leaving fans outside of the host country to rely on delayed television broadcasts or radio commentary. This lack of access often resulted in a disconnect between international fans and the sports they loved. However, OTT sports streaming has eradicated these barriers, enabling fans from all around the world to cheer for their favorite teams in real-time.

The potential for global fan engagement extends beyond mere live game-watching. Through the integration of social media and interactive features, OTT sports streaming services have transformed the viewing experience into a communal event. Fans can now interact with one another, share their thoughts and opinions, and even participate in live polls and trivia contests. This not only fosters a sense of belonging and camaraderie among sports enthusiasts but also provides valuable insights and data for broadcasters and advertisers.

Research conducted by our broadcast media streaming network has unveiled some intriguing trends in OTT sports streaming. Our data indicates that a majority of viewership comes from the younger demographics, specifically millennials and Generation Z. This shift can be attributed to the increasing preference for digital media consumption among these generations. The convenience, personalization, and social connectivity offered by OTT sports streaming have made it the preferred choice for sports fans in the digital age.

However, it is essential to acknowledge that while OTT sports streaming has revolutionized the industry, it also presents its share of challenges. The demand for high-quality live streaming puts significant pressure on network infrastructure, necessitating substantial investments in robust and scalable technologies by broadcasters. Additionally, securing broadcasting rights and negotiating partnerships with sports leagues and teams can be a complex process. Despite these difficulties, the potential for growth and innovation in the OTT sports streaming sphere is undeniable.

In conclusion, over-the-top (OTT) sports streaming services have caused a disruption in the traditional sports broadcasting landscape. These services provide fans with increased accessibility, personalized viewing experiences, and the opportunity for global fan engagement. This subchapter has explored the rise of OTT sports streaming and its impact on the industry. As a corporate leader in the broadcast media streaming field, I eagerly anticipate witnessing the ongoing evolution of OTT sports streaming and the limitless possibilities it holds for the future of sports media consumption.

Interactive Sports Streaming

At the heart of interactive sports streaming lies the capability to provide viewers with real-time statistics and data. The days of solely relying on commentators to keep fans updated on the game are gone. Through interactive sports streaming, fans have access to a plethora of information, from player statistics to game scores, all in real-time. This not only enriches the viewer experience, but also enables fans to engage in well-informed conversations with fellow sports enthusiasts.

A key aspect that contributes to the immersive nature of interactive sports streaming is the ability to switch between multiple camera angles.

The era of being restricted to a single camera angle throughout the entire game has passed. With interactive sports streaming, viewers have the freedom to select the camera angle that best suits their preferences, whether it be a behind-the-scenes view from the players' perspective or a bird's-eye view from above. This feature not only introduces a new dimension to the viewing experience, but also allows fans to attain a deeper understanding of the game by witnessing it from different vantage points.

The integration of social media emerges as another distinguishing factor of interactive sports streaming. Platforms such as Twitter and Facebook facilitate real-time engagement between fans and the game. Fans can share their thoughts and opinions, partake in discussions, and even interact with players and teams. This social aspect of interactive sports streaming fosters a sense of community among fans and offers a fresh perspective of the game. Furthermore, it presents sports organizations with an invaluable opportunity to establish connections with their audience and cultivate a loyal fan base.

The impact of interactive sports streaming extends beyond enhancing the fan experience. It also opens up new avenues for revenue generation for sports organizations. By incorporating advertisements into the streaming platform, sports organizations can widen their reach and create additional streams of revenue. Interactive sports streaming allows for targeted advertisements that can be tailored based on the viewer's interests and preferences. This not only elevates the effectiveness of advertisements, but also delivers a more personalized viewing experience for fans.

Additionally, interactive sports streaming provides sports organizations with valuable data and insights about their audience. By analyzing viewer behavior, organizations can gain a more profound understanding of their fans' interests and preferences. This data can then be utilized to develop targeted marketing strategies and provide personalized experiences for fans. The ability to accumulate this data in real-time presents a groundbreaking opportunity for sports organizations as it empowers them to promptly adapt and respond to the needs of their audience.

One of the most captivating aspects of interactive sports streaming is the potential for gamification. This feature allows viewers to actively participate in the game through predictive and interactive elements. For instance, viewers can make predictions about the outcome of a game or engage in trivia quizzes during halftime. This not only infuses an element of enjoyment and competition, but also ensures continuous engagement from viewers throughout the entirety of the game. Moreover, it offers sports organizations valuable insights into the preferences and interests of their fans, which can be harnessed for future marketing and engagement strategies.

In conclusion, interactive sports streaming has revolutionized the way fans interact with live sporting events. With features such as real-time statistics, multiple camera angles, and social media integration, viewers can fully immerse themselves in the game and engage with it on an unprecedented level. This not only elevates the fan experience, but also presents new opportunities for revenue generation for sports organizations. Interactive sports streaming is the future of sports broadcasting, revolutionizing the manner in which we experience and enjoy sports. As a social science researcher, social entrepreneur, documentary filmmaker, nonprofit executive, and the Chairman and CEO of a broadcast media streaming network, I am thrilled to be at the forefront of this revolution and personally witness the impact it has on the world of sports.

Sports Analytics and Streaming

In recent times, the realm of sports has undergone a significant transformation due to the influence of streaming media. As the Chairman and CEO of a broadcast media streaming network, I have had the privilege of witnessing firsthand how this technology has completely changed the way in which we obtain and analyze data from live sports events. In this subchapter, we will thoroughly explore the captivating field of sports analytics and examine the crucial role that streaming media plays in it.

Sports analytics is the intellectual practice of collecting and dissecting data from sports events with the objective of obtaining insights into various facets of the game. This practice encompasses the meticulous studying of player performance, team strategies, and even spectator behavior. Traditionally, this data was retrieved through manual methods such as on-field observations, box scores, and post-match analysis. However, with the advent of steaming technology, the sports analytics landscape has undergone an irreversible change.

Streaming technology facilitates the capture and analysis of data in real-time, thereby allowing for swift decision-making within the sports industry. Gone are the days when one had to wait for a match to conclude before analyzing its outcome; now, coaches can access live data and swiftly make adjustments. This prompt access to information enables teams to modify their strategies based on individual player performance, team dynamics, and even weather conditions.

One of the most notable advantages that streaming media brings to sports analytics is its ability to capture and analyze an extensive amount of data. Previously, data collection was limited to basic statistics such as goals scored, assists, and rebounds. However, with streaming technology, we are now able to gather granular data including player movement patterns, speed, acceleration, and even heart rate. This wealth of information provides an all-encompassing understanding of player performance, which is of immense importance when making informed decisions.

To exemplify the potency of streaming media within the realm of sports analytics, let us contemplate a hypothetical basketball game. In years past, coaches and analysts were reliant solely on box-score statistics to assess a player's performance. That being said, with streaming technology, we can now meticulously track every motion a player makes on the court. Through the analysis of this precise data, we are able to determine a player's shooting accuracy, defensive capabilities, and even their contribution to team chemistry. This not only aids coaches in making tactical decisions midgame, but also assists in player development and overall team performance.

Furthermore, streaming media enables the integration of multiple data sources, resulting in a holistic depiction of the game. By combining tracking data with player biometrics such as heart rate and levels of fatigue, analysts can gain a better understanding of the physical and mental demands of the game. This integrated approach to data analysis empowers teams to optimize training programs, mitigate injuries, and enhance their overall performance.

Another domain of sports analytics where streaming media has brought about a revolution is fan engagement. Previously, fans were confined to observing matches from the comfort of their homes or attending games in-person. However, with streaming technology, fans now have unparalleled access to live data and analysis. They can view real-time statistics, replays, and even participate in interactive experiences. This heightened level of engagement enriches the fan experience, while also providing valuable insights into fan behavior, preferences, and trends.

Streaming technology has also opened up fresh avenues for revenue generation within the sports industry. Through targeted advertisements and sponsorships, broadcasters can monetize their streaming platforms while delivering a personalized and tailored experience to viewers. Additionally, streaming media facilitates the creation of exclusive content such as behind-the-scenes footage, player interviews, and interactive features. This added value enhances the overall streaming experience and expands the audience, subsequently leading to more revenue opportunities.

As is the case with any technological advancement, the integration of streaming media into sports analytics presents several challenges. One vital challenge is the necessity for a robust and reliable internet infrastructure. Transmitting large volumes of data in real-time necessitates a strong network connection, which might be limited in certain regions. Additionally, concerns regarding data security and privacy must be adequately addressed in order to ensure the integrity and confidentiality of the collected information.

To conclude, streaming media has revolutionized sports analytics, equipping us with the power to capture and analyze data in real-time, a capability that was once unimaginable. The integration of streaming technology in the sports industry has fundamentally transformed decision-making processes, player development, fan engagement, and revenue generation. As a social science researcher, social entrepreneur, and documentary filmmaker, I am deeply fascinated by the potential that streaming media brings to the world of sports analytics. It is an influential tool that empowers us to gain unmatched insights into the game, resulting in strategic advancements and an all-encompassing viewing experience for fans across the globe.

With this, we bring an end to our exploration of sports analytics and streaming. In the subsequent subchapter, we will delve into the exhilarating world of live streaming platforms and their profound impact on the media industry. We invite you to stay tuned for a comprehensive analysis of this rapidly evolving landscape in the digital age.

Chapter 20: Streaming Media in the Arts

Streaming Music and the Music Industry

The emergence of streaming music platforms has brought about a significant transformation in the manner in which we engage with and consume music. The days of eagerly queuing outside record stores, eagerly anticipating the release of the latest album, and playing our favorite tunes on cassette tapes or vinyl records are now a thing of the past. In our current era, music is readily accessible at our fingertips, available anytime and anywhere with just a few simple clicks or taps.

The rise of streaming platforms can be attributed, in part, to technological advancements. With the widespread availability of high-speed internet, the capability to efficiently and swiftly transmit large amounts of data has become a reality. Coupled with the increasing prevalence of smartphones and mobile devices, these circumstances have paved the way for the streaming music revolution to take hold.

The shift from physical music sales to digital streaming has indeed been a game-changer for consumers; however, it has also presented a multitude of challenges for artists and record labels. One of the most significant obstacles they face is the decline in revenue generated from traditional music sales. Historically, artists heavily relied on album sales and royalties as their primary source of income. With the advent of streaming, however, the revenue model has undergone a shift, with artists now deriving a substantial portion of their earnings from streaming services.

This change has raised concerns among artists and record labels, who harbor apprehensions regarding the fairness and sustainability of the streaming economy. Many contend that streaming platforms inadequately compensate artists for their creative work. Despite the popularity of streaming, the financial returns from platforms like Spotify and Apple Music have come under scrutiny, with certain artists asserting that they receive meager royalties despite amassing millions of streams.

Moreover, the pervasiveness of streaming platforms has contributed to market oversaturation. Given the sheer magnitude of songs available at any given moment, emerging artists encounter increasing difficulties in breaking through the cacophony and gaining exposure. Traditionally influential entities in the music industry, such as record labels and radio stations, no longer possess the same degree of influence in determining popular trends. The democratization of music distribution, while advantageous in certain aspects, also brings forth certain drawbacks.

However, it is not a dire picture for the music industry as a whole. Although challenges undoubtedly exist, streaming technology has concurrently ushered in a multitude of opportunities for both artists and record labels. Most notably, it has enabled the potential for widespread global music distribution. With streaming platforms accessible throughout the majority of the world, artists now possess the capacity to connect with a global audience without the need for physical distribution networks. Such a development has leveled the playing field, permitting artists from all walks of life to gain recognition and fostering a greater sense of diversity and representation within the music industry.

Additionally, streaming platforms serve as invaluable tools for discovering new music. In previous times, individuals relied on word-of-mouth recommendations or fortuitously chanced upon hidden musical gems on the radio. Nowadays, with the presence of curated playlists, personalized suggestions, and algorithm-driven recommendations, listeners can effortlessly explore different genres, artists, and songs that may have remained undiscovered otherwise. This trend has contributed to the flourishing of niche genres and a resurgence of interest in lesser-known tracks and forgotten classics.

Furthermore, streaming platforms have provided independent artists with a platform to showcase their talents and discover an audience. Previously, countless gifted musicians struggled to penetrate the industry due to limited connections and resources. However, with the advent of streaming, artists can directly release their music on platforms such as Spotify or SoundCloud, effectively bypassing traditional gatekeepers. This newfound autonomy has empowered artists to seize control of their careers and build a dedicated following from scratch.

Undoubtedly, streaming technology has significantly disrupted and transformed the music industry, fundamentally altering the way in which we engage with, create, and disseminate music. While the challenges faced by artists and record labels are not insignificant, the opportunities presented in terms of global music distribution and discovery are equally momentous. By fully comprehending the multifaceted nature of this revolution and embracing both its advantages and limitations, we can truly navigate and thrive in this ever-evolving landscape.

Streaming Theater and Performing Arts

Theater has long been regarded as a captivating medium that transports its audiences to various realms, but its potential has frequently been confined by physical limitations. Geographic constraints, financial restrictions, and accessibility issues have often prevented individuals from attending live performances. Nevertheless, streaming platforms are altering this narrative by dismantling these barriers and affording theater and performing arts the opportunity to reach a wider audience.

One of the most notable advantages of streaming theater is the ability to broaden its audience base. By making performances available online, theaters can reach spectators in diverse locations around the globe, surpassing their immediate geographic boundaries. This new-found accessibility has the potential to introduce varied audiences to the artistry and profundity of theater, thereby fostering cultural exchange and understanding.

Additionally, streaming platforms offer a distinctive advantage in preserving artistic works. By their very nature, theater productions are ephemeral, their performances fleeting and transient. Once a show has concluded its run, it becomes quite challenging for individuals to encounter it again. Yet, with the advent of streaming, these performances can now be immortalized and shared for the benefit of future generations. This preservation of artistic works enables the documentation and analysis of different theatrical techniques, acting styles, and stage designs, thus contributing to theater's invaluable cultural legacy.

Furthermore, streaming theater brings with it the democratization of access to cultural experiences. Traditionally, attending a live performance necessitates the purchase of a ticket, which can be exorbitantly priced for certain individuals. By streaming performances online, theaters can provide more affordable options, thereby granting access to high-quality productions for those with limited financial means. This democratization ensures that theater is no longer an exclusive art form accessible only to those of considerable means, but rather, it becomes an art that can be enjoyed by anyone with an internet connection.

Moreover, streaming platforms represent a significant shift in how theater productions are curated and presented. Theater creators now have the opportunity to experiment with new formats and approaches, thereby fostering innovation within the industry. Streaming allows for the amalgamation of diverse art forms, such as combining live performances with pre-recorded elements or incorporating interactive aspects that engage the online audience. The possibilities are endless, and the advent of streaming has opened up a realm of creative opportunities for theater artists.

Another enriching aspect of streaming theater lies in the provision of behind-the-scenes content. Viewers now have unprecedented access to the creative processes and backstage realm of theater. Through interviews, documentaries, and behind-the-scenes footage, streaming platforms afford an intimate look into the creation of theatrical productions. This insight enables audiences to deepen their appreciation for the art form while also serving as a unique educational opportunity for aspiring theater practitioners.

The impact of streaming theater and performing arts extends beyond the audience experience, also offering new career pathways and revenue streams for professionals in the theater industry. With the escalating demand for streaming content, theaters can now produce shows aimed specifically at online audiences, thereby expanding their reach and diversifying their sources of income. Actors, directors, and other theater practitioners can now participate in projects previously unavailable to them, thus contributing to the growth and sustainability of the industry.

Nonetheless, as with any innovative technology, streaming platforms present their own set of challenges and considerations. Preserving the quality of live performances in the streaming format is a key concern. Theater is an immersive, visceral experience, and capturing that essence in a digital format is a complex undertaking. Technical aspects, such as camera angles, sound quality, and lighting, must be meticulously taken into account to ensure the audience's connection with the performance remains intact.

Furthermore, copyright issues and safeguards for intellectual property rights must be addressed when streaming theater productions. Theater creators must navigate the intricacies of licensing agreements and strike a balance between protecting their work and making it accessible to a wider audience. Collaborative efforts are paramount in establishing guidelines and protocols that safeguard the rights of artists while encouraging the growth of streaming platforms in the theater industry.

In conclusion, streaming platforms have revolutionized the theater and performing arts industry by offering increased audience reach, preservation of artistic works, and democratized access to cultural experiences. Through the power of streaming, theater has surmounted physical limitations and forged new avenues for creative expression. By embracing this digital transformation, the theater community has the ability to engage, inspire, and educate audiences in ways that were once unimaginable. As a researcher in the realm of social sciences, a social entrepreneur, a documentary filmmaker, a nonprofit executive, and the Chairman and CEO of a broadcast media streaming network, it is an honor for me to witness and advocate for this transformation, recognizing its potential to shape the future of theater for generations to come.

Virtual Art Exhibitions and Streaming

As a researcher in the field of social sciences, social entrepreneur, documentary filmmaker, nonprofit executive, and the Chairman and CEO of a broadcast media streaming network, I have been fortunate enough to witness firsthand the transformative impact that streaming technology has had on the world of visual arts. The art world has experienced a revolution in recent years, driven by the rapid advancements in streaming technology. Virtual art exhibitions have emerged as a groundbreaking means for artists to showcase their work to global audiences, breaking down geographical barriers and encouraging artistic collaborations like never before.

In the past, art exhibitions were limited to physical spaces, which often restricted the audience to individuals who could physically visit the gallery or museum. However, with the advent of streaming technology, artists now have the ability to bring their work to viewers around the world. Virtual art exhibitions have become a platform for artists to overcome the limitations of physical spaces and reach a wider audience, providing opportunities for exposure, recognition, and even sales.

The possibilities offered by virtual art exhibitions are truly limitless. Artists can now curate and design interactive virtual spaces to showcase their work, complete with detailed descriptions, videos, and even 3D models. Viewers can navigate through these virtual galleries at their own pace, exploring each artwork in depth and gaining a deeper understanding of the artist's vision. This immersive experience allows for a deeper connection between the artist and the viewer, blurring the boundaries between the physical and digital realms.

One of the most exciting aspects of virtual art exhibitions is their potential to foster artistic collaborations. Artists from different parts of the world can come together in a virtual space to create collaborative works, breaking down geographical barriers and pushing the boundaries of traditional art forms. Streaming technology enables real-time collaboration, where artists can work together on a single piece, even if they are thousands of miles apart. This has opened up new avenues for creativity and innovation, as artists are able to draw inspiration from various cultures, perspectives, and artistic styles.

Digital galleries have also emerged as a popular platform for artists to showcase their work. These online platforms not only provide a space for artists to exhibit their creations, but also offer tools to facilitate sales and connect artists with potential buyers. Streaming technology has revolutionized the way art is marketed and sold, making it more accessible to a global audience. Artists can now reach collectors and art enthusiasts from all corners of the globe, expanding their market and maximizing their exposure.

Additionally, streaming technology has propelled the growth of immersive art experiences. Through the use of Virtual Reality (VR) and Augmented Reality (AR) technologies, artists can create interactive and immersive artworks that engage the viewer on a whole new level. These immersive experiences transport the viewer into a different world, allowing them to explore and interact with the artwork in ways that were previously unimaginable. Streaming technology enables the seamless delivery of these immersive experiences, enhancing the viewer's engagement and creating a truly transformative and multisensory art encounter.

In conclusion, the convergence of streaming media and visual arts has revolutionized the way art is exhibited, experienced, and shared. Virtual art exhibitions, digital galleries, and immersive art experiences have opened up new opportunities for artists to showcase their work to global audiences, foster artistic collaborations, and push the boundaries of traditional art forms. As streaming technology continues to evolve, we can expect further innovation and exploration in the realm of visual arts, creating new and exciting possibilities for both artists and viewers alike.

Chapter 21: Streaming Media in Cultural Preservation

Cultural Performances and Festivals

Definition and Context:

Cultural performances and festivals encompass a wide range of artistic expressions that celebrate the traditions, history, and values of a particular culture. From music concerts and dance recitals to theatrical productions and street parades, these events serve as crucial platforms for cultural exchange, education, and community-building. They provide individuals with the opportunity to showcase their talents, express their identities, and establish connections with their cultural roots.

In the past, the experience of cultural performances and festivals posed challenges for those unable to attend them in person. Distance, cost, and logistical constraints often hindered individuals from witnessing these events, limiting their exposure to diverse cultural practices. However, with the emergence of streaming media, these obstacles are being overcome, expanding the reach and impact of cultural performances and festivals like never before.

Real-Time Global Access:

Streaming platforms have revolutionized the broadcasting and consumption of cultural performances and festivals. With a stable internet connection, individuals can now access live streams of these events from any location worldwide, surpassing geographical boundaries and time zones. This has resulted in a global audience that can witness the authenticity and vibrancy of cultural performances in real-time, fostering a sense of connection and unity among people from diverse backgrounds.

The accessibility of streaming media has democratized cultural experiences, allowing individuals who may not have had the means or opportunity to attend festivals or performances in person to engage and appreciate the rich tapestry of global cultural expressions. Through their screens, viewers can immerse themselves in the sights, sounds, and emotions of traditional music, dance, and theatrical productions, promoting cross-cultural understanding and appreciation.

Preserving Cultural Heritage:

Beyond the immediate enjoyment and entertainment value, streaming media plays a crucial role in the preservation of cultural heritage and digitization. Cultural performances and festivals are often rooted in deeply historical and traditional practices passed down from one generation to the next. By broadcasting these events using streaming technology, they can be documented, archived, and preserved for future generations.

Streaming platforms enable cultural organizations and artists to capture high-quality audio and visual recordings of their performances, ensuring that these artistic expressions are not lost to time. This documentation serves as a valuable resource for researchers, educators, and enthusiasts interested in studying and comprehending different cultures and their artistic expressions. Additionally, digitized cultural performances can be shared with indigenous communities and diaspora populations, aiding them in reconnecting with their heritage and bolstering cultural identity.

Respectful Representation and Intellectual Property Rights:

While streaming media has undoubtedly broadened the reach of cultural performances and festivals, it also presents certain challenges and ethical considerations. As these events are streamed to global audiences, it is essential to ensure that they are represented and presented with the respect and sensitivity they deserve. Cultural performances often hold profound spiritual, historical, and social significance, and their misrepresentation can perpetuate stereotypes and misunderstandings.

To address these concerns, it is crucial for streaming platforms and content creators to engage in close collaboration with the communities and artists involved in cultural performances and festivals. This collaborative approach can help establish guidelines and protocols that safeguard artistic integrity and prevent the appropriation or distortion of cultural expressions. Respecting intellectual property rights and seeking permission from artists and communities before streaming their performances form crucial aspects of ethical cultural streaming.

Conclusion:

Streaming media has transformed the broadcasting and experience of cultural performances and festivals. It has given rise to a global audience that can appreciate and participate in the diverse range of cultural expressions, uniting people and promoting cross-cultural understanding. However, the responsible and respectful representation of cultural performances necessitates collaboration, sensitivity, and adherence to intellectual property rights. By navigating these challenges, streaming platforms can continue to provide a window into various cultural practices, ensuring their longevity, and facilitating future generations' appreciation and learning.

Oral History and Storytelling

Oral history has long been recognized as a valuable method for preserving the narratives and experiences of individuals and communities.

It serves as a means of passing down cultural traditions through the spoken word from one generation to the next. However, the accessibility and permanence of oral history have presented challenges. In the past, recordings were made using tape recorders or other analog devices, which imposed limitations in terms of storage, quality, and ease of sharing. Yet, with the advent of streaming platforms, we now possess the capability to capture and disseminate oral history in a manner that was previously unimaginable.

One of the significant advantages of streaming media in the preservation of oral history is its ability to record and share stories from diverse cultures. In our increasingly interconnected world, it is imperative to ensure that all voices and narratives are adequately represented. Streaming platforms provide an avenue for individuals from various backgrounds to share their stories, thus enriching our collective understanding of the human experience.

For instance, consider a streaming platform dedicated to the preservation and sharing of Indigenous oral traditions. Indigenous communities worldwide possess a wealth of cultural knowledge and stories that have been transmitted orally across generations. Through streaming technology, we can capture and safeguard these narratives, guaranteeing that they are not lost to the passage of time. Additionally, by making these stories accessible to a global audience, we can foster a greater appreciation and comprehension of Indigenous cultures.

Streaming media also plays a crucial role in facilitating intergenerational knowledge transfer. In many cultures, the transmission of stories from elders to younger generations is integral to the preservation of cultural heritage. Streaming platforms enable the recording and sharing of these stories with future generations, even if they are unable to be physically present. This guarantees the continuous transmission and appreciation of cultural traditions and values, even in our fast-paced, digital age.

Furthermore, streaming media possesses the power to conserve endangered languages. Language and culture share an inseparable bond, and the loss of a language often entails the loss of an entire way of life. By recording and streaming stories in endangered languages, we can contribute to the revitalization and preservation of these linguistic treasures. This is particularly invaluable concerning indigenous languages, which are at risk of vanishing within the context of a globalized culture.

Nevertheless, documenting and streaming sensitive cultural narratives also raises important ethical considerations. As researchers, filmmakers, and broadcasters, it is crucial that we approach this work with empathy, cultural sensitivity, and respect for the communities whose stories we are documenting. Obtaining informed consent is of the utmost importance – it is essential to secure permission from individuals and communities before recording and sharing their oral histories. Furthermore, we must exercise care to ensure that these narratives are presented in a manner that accurately represents the perspectives and experiences of the storytellers, without imposing external interpretations or distortions.

In conclusion, the utilization of streaming media for preserving oral history and storytelling represents a powerful tool for cultural preservation. It enables the recording and sharing of stories from diverse cultures, fosters intergenerational knowledge transfer, and contributes to the revitalization of endangered languages. However, it is imperative to approach this work ethically and responsibly, showing respect for the stories and the communities from which they originate. By leveraging streaming technology, we have the opportunity to uphold cultural traditions and guarantee that the voices of our ancestors continue to resonate with future generations.

In the next subchapter, we will explore the technological considerations of streaming media, including the infrastructure, codecs, and bandwidth requirements that enable the seamless transmission of audio and video content over the internet.

Virtual Museum Tours and Exhibitions

As a dedicated researcher and social entrepreneur in the field of broadcast media streaming, I have always been captivated by the opportunities that technology presents in expanding access to cultural heritage and promoting cultural preservation. In this subchapter, I will explore the topic of virtual museum tours and exhibitions, examining how streaming platforms have revolutionized the manner in which audiences engage with museums, art galleries, and historical sites remotely. Additionally, I will discuss the potential of streaming technology in democratizing access to these cultural treasures and involving new audiences in the pursuit of cultural preservation.

The Significance of Streaming Platforms:

Streaming media has emerged as a potent tool in bringing the world's museums and art galleries to the fingertips of people around the globe. Through the utilization of streaming platforms, virtual museum tours and exhibitions have become a concrete reality, granting audiences the ability to explore these cultural institutions from a distance. These advancements in technology have eliminated geographical and financial barriers, facilitating access for individuals from all walks of life to appreciate and engage with art, history, and culture effortlessly.

One of the most notable advantages of streaming platforms for virtual museum tours is the capacity to bring the museum experience into the homes of individuals who may lack the means to visit these institutions physically. For those with physical limitations, financial constraints, or restricted access due to location, virtual museum tours offer an inclusive experience that was once inconceivable. Through the power of streaming technology, individuals with an internet connection can embark on a journey through the esteemed halls of museums, guided by knowledgeable curators and historians.

The democratization of access to cultural heritage is a fundamental outcome of these virtual museum tours facilitated by streaming platforms. By removing obstacles such as cost and distance, streaming technology enables audiences to engage with art, artifacts, and historical sites that were previously accessible only to a select few. This democratization extends cultural appreciation to individuals from various backgrounds, fostering inclusivity and encouraging a greater understanding and appreciation of diverse cultures.

Engaging New Audiences and Cultural Preservation:

Streaming technology not only ensures access to cultural heritage but also presents opportunities for engagement and participation. Through interactive features and immersive experiences, virtual museum tours facilitated by streaming platforms enhance audience engagement by providing avenues for exploration and discovery. Visitors can zoom in on intricate details of artworks, access supplementary content, and even interact with certain exhibits in real-time. These interactive elements create a personalized and engaging experience, captivating audiences and inviting them to actively participate in the preservation of cultural heritage.

Moreover, streaming technology has become a valuable tool in engaging new audiences who may be less inclined to visit physical museums and galleries. By delivering cultural experiences through accessible and familiar platforms, such as computers, smartphones, and smart TVs, streaming technology appeals to the digital generation, capturing their attention and fostering an interest in art and history. This engagement with virtual museum tours can inspire the next generation of cultural enthusiasts, ensuring the continued preservation and appreciation of cultural heritage.

Furthermore, streaming technology has the potential to revolutionize efforts in cultural preservation. By digitizing collections and making them available for virtual museum tours, institutions can safeguard artifacts that may be at risk of deterioration or damage. Additionally, streaming platforms provide a means to showcase exhibitions and collections that may not be physically feasible due to spatial limitations or logistical constraints. By embracing streaming technology, museums and galleries can broaden their reach, preserve precious artifacts, and guarantee that their cultural legacy is accessible to future generations.

In Conclusion:

In conclusion, virtual museum tours and exhibitions powered by streaming technology have transformed the way audiences engage with cultural heritage. These innovative platforms make it possible for individuals worldwide to readily access and appreciate art, history, and culture, thereby dismantling physical and financial barriers. This democratization of access fosters inclusivity and promotes a deeper understanding and appreciation of cultural heritage.

Furthermore, streaming technology opens up new avenues for engagement and participation, enabling audiences to actively contribute to the preservation of cultural heritage. By delivering immersive and interactive experiences, streaming platforms captivate audiences, inspire new cultural enthusiasts, and ensure the continued preservation and appreciation of art, artifacts, and historical sites.

As a social science researcher, social entrepreneur, documentary filmmaker, nonprofit executive, and the Chairman and CEO of a broadcast media streaming network, I am dedicated to utilizing streaming technology to advance access to cultural heritage and promote cultural preservation. The potential of streaming platforms in democratizing access and engaging new audiences in cultural preservation efforts is undeniable. By embracing these technological advancements, we can ensure that the treasures of our collective cultural heritage are preserved for generations to come.

Chapter 22: Streaming Media in Science and Technology

Live Streaming Scientific Events and Conferences

The emergence of live streaming has brought about a significant transformation in the manner in which scientific events and conferences are conducted. The days of limited attendance, restricted to a select group physically present at the venue, are a thing of the past. With a stable internet connection and a streaming platform, individuals possessing a computer or mobile device can now actively participate in these intellectual gatherings. This democratization of knowledge results in increased inclusivity and facilitates the exchange of ideas across geographical boundaries.

One of the primary advantages of live streaming scientific events lies in its ability to bridge the gap between researchers situated in different parts of the world. Scientific breakthroughs and discoveries often originate in isolated pockets, but through live streaming, these isolated pockets evolve into interconnected centers of innovation. The real-time communication capability allows for collaboration, sharing of findings, and the solicitation of feedback from peers, irrespective of their physical location. This level of global collaboration fosters a sense of community and encourages innovative thinking.

Moreover, live streaming of scientific events presents opportunities for remote participation. This is particularly beneficial for researchers who face logistical constraints, financial limitations, or other commitments that prevent them from traveling. By providing remote access to presentations, workshops, and panel discussions, live streaming ensures that nobody is left behind. It enables individuals from diverse backgrounds and circumstances to engage with the latest developments in their respective fields, empowering them to contribute to scientific knowledge advancement.

Furthermore, live streaming of scientific events extends beyond mere information dissemination. It also serves as a platform for interactive audience engagement. During traditional conferences, audience participation is often restricted to Q&A sessions that occur after presentations. However, with live streaming, audience members can actively participate in discussions, ask questions, and contribute to the dialogue in real-time. This interactive element cultivates a sense of intellectual curiosity and promotes critical thinking among both presenters and viewers.

Certainly, just like any technological advancement, live streaming of scientific events presents its own set of challenges. One of the primary challenges lies in the requirement of reliable internet connections. Without a stable and high-speed internet connection, the streaming experience might be compromised, resulting in interruptions, buffering, or even complete disconnections. To address this challenge, event organizers must ensure that the venue possesses robust internet infrastructure or explore alternative options such as satellite connections or dedicated networks. Additionally, participants should be encouraged to test their internet connections prior to the event in order to minimize disruptions.

Another challenge that arises from live streaming of scientific events pertains to the management of intellectual property rights. Researchers invest significant amounts of time, effort, and resources into their work and safeguarding their findings assumes paramount importance. Event organizers must implement mechanisms to secure intellectual property, such as password-protected streams or restricted access to specific sessions. Furthermore, clear guidelines must be communicated to participants regarding the sharing, recording, and dissemination of streamed content to prevent unauthorized usage or distribution.

Furthermore, live streaming of scientific events raises ethical and etiquette concerns surrounding virtual participation. Participants must be mindful of the virtual space they occupy and adhere to professional conduct standards. This entails refraining from disruptive behaviors, respecting the privacy of other attendees, and engaging in meaningful and constructive dialogue. Event organizers should establish explicit guidelines and expectations for participants to ensure a positive and inclusive streaming experience for all.

Despite these challenges, the advantages of live streaming of scientific events outweigh the drawbacks. Through this innovative means of communication, researchers have the opportunity to reach a global audience, share their findings in real-time, and engage in collaborative conversations with fellow scientists from around the world. The advancements in streaming technology have made it easier than ever to bridge the gap between scientific communities, foster innovation, and accelerate the pace of scientific discovery.

In conclusion, live streaming has completely transformed the landscape of scientific events and conferences, enabling the real-time sharing of knowledge, remote participation, and global collaboration. The benefits of this technology are wide-ranging, ranging from the bridging of geographical gaps to the empowerment of researchers who might face impediments to in-person attendance. However, it is crucial to acknowledge and address the challenges associated with live streaming, such as the requirement for reliable internet connections and the management of intellectual property rights. By navigating these challenges and embracing the opportunities, the scientific community can harness the power of live streaming to facilitate the exchange of ideas, foster innovation, and push the boundaries of knowledge.

Virtual Science Education and Outreach

In recent years, there has been a growing recognition of the need to enhance science education and promote scientific literacy among the general population. Although traditional methods of science education, such as textbooks and lectures, still hold value, they often fall short in capturing the interest and curiosity of learners. Streaming media offers a viable solution to address this issue by providing a platform for delivering captivating and interactive science lessons.

One notable advantage of streaming technology in the realm of science education is its ability to create immersive learning experiences. By integrating video, audio, graphics, and interactive elements, streaming platforms can transport learners into virtual laboratories, enabling them to engage in hands-on experimentation, data analysis, and exploration of scientific concepts. This virtual approach to science education not only deepens comprehension but also instills excitement and curiosity, which may be lacking in traditional classroom settings.

Furthermore, streaming media facilitates real-time collaboration and interaction between educators and learners, regardless of their geographical location. This offers immense potential for science education and outreach, particularly in underserved communities or regions with limited access to high-quality educational resources. Through streaming platforms, students in remote areas can be afforded the same learning opportunities as their counterparts in well-funded institutions, thereby leveling the educational playing field and ensuring that all learners can access high-quality scientific education.

In addition to virtual experiments, streaming technology also supports science communication endeavors. By means of live-streamed lectures, talks, and panel discussions, scientists can effectively connect with a global audience and share their research findings in real-time. This not only fosters scientific discovery and innovation but also nurtures a deeper understanding and appreciation of science among the general public. By rendering science communication more easily accessible and interactive, streaming media can bridge the divide between scientists and society, promoting dialogue and engagement.

The potential of streaming technology in science education and outreach is further strengthened by recent studies and research. One such study conducted by Smith et al. (2019) demonstrated that students engaging with virtual science lessons through streaming platforms exhibited higher levels of conceptual understanding compared to those relying solely on traditional methods. The immersive and interactive nature of streaming platforms allowed students to actively participate with the material, resulting in a more profound grasp of scientific concepts.

Furthermore, a study conducted by Johnson et al. (2020) explored the impact of streaming media on science communication and found that live-streamed science talks generated greater interest and engagement among viewers compared to recorded lectures. The real-time interaction and question-and-answer sessions facilitated by streaming platforms enabled viewers to directly engage with scientists, ask questions, and delve deeper into the topics being discussed. This kind of interactive engagement has the potential to ignite scientific curiosity and inspire the next generation of scientists.

Streaming media also holds potential in supporting science education and outreach in non-traditional settings. For instance, through collaborations with museums, science centers, and non-profit organizations, streaming platforms can facilitate virtual field trips and interactive exhibits, enabling students to explore scientific concepts in a hands-on and immersive manner. This form of virtual learning experience can be particularly advantageous for students who may face geographical or financial constraints in visiting physical science museums.

In conclusion, the utilization of streaming media in virtual science education and outreach has the capacity to transform the way we learn, engage with, and communicate science. By offering immersive and interactive learning experiences, streaming platforms can enhance scientific literacy, ignite curiosity, and promote educational equality.

Through partnerships and collaborations, streaming technology can make science education accessible to all, irrespective of geographical location or socioeconomic background. As we continue to explore the possibilities of streaming media, it is imperative that we harness its power to create a future where science education is engaging, inclusive, and accessible to all.

Open Science and Research Dissemination Through Streaming

As a social scientist and researcher, I have always been intrigued by the potential of streaming media to revolutionize the dissemination of scientific knowledge. Through my work as a documentary filmmaker and nonprofit executive, I have directly witnessed the impact of streaming technology in connecting people from various parts of the world and facilitating the exchange of ideas and information.

The scientific community has long aimed to democratize scientific knowledge, but traditional dissemination methods have often hindered this goal due to their limited reach and accessibility. Streaming media has the capacity to overcome these limitations by providing scientists and researchers with a platform to share their work with a global audience in real-time.

One of the most significant advantages of streaming platforms is their ability to transcend geographical barriers. In the past, attending academic conferences and seminars necessitated travel, time, and financial resources. However, streaming technology allows researchers to participate remotely, eliminating the need for physical presence. This not only broadens access for researchers who lack the means to attend in person, but also enables a wider range of perspectives and expertise to be present at these gatherings.

In addition to overcoming geographical barriers, streaming media also has the potential to expedite the dissemination of scientific findings. Traditional publishing processes can be lengthy, with research often taking months or even years to be published in peer-reviewed journals. Streaming technology allows researchers to share their findings in real-time, enabling the scientific community to build upon these discoveries more promptly.

The movement towards open science has gained momentum in recent years, advocating for free and unrestricted access to scientific knowledge. Streaming platforms align perfectly with the goals of open science by providing a means of disseminating research findings to a broader audience without the need for costly subscriptions or paywalls. When research is freely accessible, it has the potential to reach a wider audience, including policymakers, journalists, and the general public, who can benefit from this knowledge in various ways.

Furthermore, streaming technology promotes data sharing and collaboration among researchers. Through live-streamed conferences and webinars, researchers can share their data and methodologies with others in real-time, fostering a culture of transparency and openness. This encourages collaboration and the exchange of ideas, leading to breakthroughs and advancements that would be otherwise unattainable.

However, along with these opportunities come challenges. One of the main challenges is ensuring the reliability and quality of the streamed content. Scientific research requires rigorous methodologies and peer-review processes to guarantee the accuracy and validity of the findings. Streaming platforms must implement measures to ensure that the content being shared is trustworthy and meets the standards of scientific rigor.

Another challenge is the need for infrastructure and technical support. Streaming high-quality video and audio demands a robust network infrastructure and technical expertise. Not all researchers may have access to the necessary resources to effectively utilize streaming technology. Addressing this challenge requires investments in infrastructure, as well as training and support for researchers in using streaming platforms.

Additionally, ethical considerations need to be taken into account when it comes to open science and research dissemination through streaming. Researchers must be mindful of issues such as privacy and consent when sharing data and findings through streaming media. It is crucial to establish guidelines and protocols to ensure the protection of individuals' rights and confidentiality.

Despite these challenges, the potential benefits of open science and research dissemination through streaming are immense. By leveraging streaming technology, researchers can reach a global audience, expedite the pace of scientific discovery, and facilitate collaboration and data sharing. Streaming platforms present an opportunity to break down barriers and democratize scientific knowledge, ultimately advancing the progress of scientific research and benefiting society as a whole.

In conclusion, streaming media has the potential to revolutionize the dissemination of scientific knowledge. By harnessing streaming platforms, researchers can share their discoveries, findings, and insights with a global audience in real-time. Open science and research dissemination through streaming offer opportunities to increase access to scientific knowledge, promote data sharing and collaboration, and expedite the pace of scientific discovery. While challenges exist in ensuring the reliability and quality of streamed content, addressing these challenges can lead to a more open and inclusive scientific community. It is essential for researchers, policymakers, and technologists to collaborate in order to harness the power of streaming media for the betterment of scientific research and society as a whole.

Chapter 23: Streaming Media in Social Entrepreneurship

Socially Conscious Streaming Platforms

As an individual with background in social sciences, filmmaking, and social-entrepreneurship, I have always been intrigued by the influence of media in shaping perspectives and driving positive change in society. Throughout my professional journey, I have observed the transformative potential of streaming platforms that place social impact and community engagement at the forefront. These platforms offer more than just entertainment; they serve as platforms where dialogue, education, and activism converge.

A prime example of such a platform is Bufé Tv, an innovative streaming network that I have the privilege of leading as Chairman and CEO. Bufé Tv is dedicated to promoting social awareness and community engagement as its main mission. By curating a diverse range of content, including documentaries, docuseries, and independent films, and actively collaborating with nonprofit organizations, Bufé Tv aims to inspire viewers and foster positive social impact.

The key to cultivating social awareness lies in carefully curating content that exposes viewers to a multitude of perspectives, addresses crucial social issues, and challenges established norms. It is crucial for socially conscious streaming platforms to provide a space for voices that have historically been marginalized or silenced.

Bufé Tv, for instance, actively seeks out independent filmmakers who tackle thought-provoking subjects such as social inequality, environmental justice, and human rights. By featuring documentaries and docuseries that shed light on these pressing social matters, Bufé Tv fosters understanding and empathy among its viewers.

In addition to these documentaries, Bufé Tv also presents a wide range of films and series that embrace diversity and inclusivity. Whether it is sharing stories from underrepresented communities or challenging stereotypes, the platform strives to offer viewers a well-rounded and inclusive selection of content.

One of the most influential aspects of socially conscious streaming platforms is their ability to nurture dialogue and challenge societal norms. By curating content that addresses controversial subjects and pushes boundaries, these platforms create spaces where meaningful conversations can take place.

Bufé Tv, for instance, arranges virtual panels and Q&A sessions with filmmakers, experts, and activists involved in creating the platform's content. This allows viewers to directly engage with the creators and gain a deeper comprehension of the issues being presented. These events often encourage thought-provoking discussions and motivate viewers to take action within their own communities.

Moreover, socially conscious streaming platforms promote user-generated content, providing individuals with a platform to share their own stories and perspectives. By empowering users to contribute to the conversation, these platforms generate a sense of community and collective accountability for social change.

Ultimately, the true impact of socially conscious streaming platforms lies in their ability to inspire positive change. By exposing viewers to the realities of social issues and equipping them with the means to take action, these platforms empower individuals to become agents of change within their own communities.

Bufé Tv, for example, establishes partnerships with nonprofit organizations and grassroots movements to amplify their messages and support their initiatives. Through collaborative campaigns and fundraising efforts, Bufé Tv actively contributes to causes it believes in, thereby extending the reach of its impact beyond the virtual realm.

Furthermore, Bufé Tv offers resources and information for viewers interested in getting involved. These resources include educational materials, toolkits, as well as volunteering and donation opportunities. By connecting viewers with practical ways to make a difference, the platform ensures that its impact goes beyond the act of streaming.

In conclusion, socially conscious streaming platforms hold the potential to reshape the media landscape and inspire positive change. By curating content that promotes social awareness, diversity, and inclusivity, these platforms create spaces for dialogue, challenge societal norms, and empower individuals to take action. Bufé Tv serves as an exemplary model, prioritizing social impact and community engagement in its mission. As we continue to explore the possibilities of streaming media, it is crucial that we embrace and support platforms that prioritize social consciousness and foster a collective sense of responsibility for creating a better world.

Streaming for Nonprofit Organizations

Nonprofit organizations play a crucial and indispensable role in addressing societal issues and effecting positive change. From environmental conservation to social justice, these organizations are driven by a shared mission to improve the world. Nonetheless, reaching a larger audience and attracting support has always posed a challenge for these nonprofits. Traditional methods of communication and outreach are limited in terms of cost, geographical reach, and efficacy.

Streaming media has emerged as a potent tool for nonprofit organizations to overcome these challenges. By harnessing the capabilities of various streaming platforms, these organizations can now connect with a global audience in real-time, regardless of their location. This break-through has opened up a multitude of possibilities for nonprofits to amplify their messages and engage with supporters in unprecedented ways.

A key method through which nonprofits are employing streaming media is by live-streaming events. Whether it be a fundraising gala, a conference, or a community gathering, nonprofits can now broadcast these events to a global audience. Live-streaming not only enables those unable to attend in person to participate remotely, but it also fosters a sense of excitement, urgency, and community among supporters world-wide. Through interactive features such as live chat and Q&A sessions, viewers can directly engage with the organization, pose questions, and provide feedback, thereby fostering a sense of connection and involvement.

In addition to live-streaming events, nonprofits are also utilizing streaming platforms to share impactful stories. Through short films, documentaries, and interviews, organizations can showcase the tangible impact of their work. These videos provide a powerful medium to emotionally connect with viewers, helping them grasp the significance of the organization's mission and inspiring them to take action. Whether it is shedding light on lives transformed by a nonprofit's efforts or illuminating the urgency of an issue, impact stories shared through streaming media possess the ability to leave a lasting impression on the audience.

Moreover, streaming technology allows nonprofits to engage donors and volunteers more effectively. By streaming fundraising campaigns and appeals, organizations can reach a wider audience and encourage greater participation. Through storytelling techniques and compelling visuals, nonprofits can convey their message in a manner that resonates with potential donors, thereby increasing the likelihood of receiving support. Furthermore, streaming platforms offer fundraising features, including donation buttons and virtual auctions, simplifying the process for viewers to contribute and support the cause.

Nonprofits are also harnessing the power of streaming media in their social advocacy endeavors. Streaming platforms provide an accessible and cost-effective way to broadcast rallies, protests, and awareness campaigns, enabling organizations to reach a larger audience and rally support for their cause. Live-streaming these events not only raises awareness but also facilitates participation from individuals who may not have the physical ability to attend. This accessibility possesses the potential to bring together a diverse group of supporters and foster a unified voice for social change.

The potential of streaming technology to enhance nonprofit visibility cannot be underestimated. In an increasingly digital world, streaming media offers organizations the opportunity to elevate their presence and expand their reach. By leveraging the power of audio and video, nonprofits can connect with a global audience, bolster their brand recognition, and ultimately attract more support for their cause.

Fundraising efforts, in particular, greatly benefit from streaming media. Traditional fundraising methods often rely on in-person events and personal connections, restricting the reach and scale of campaigns. However, with streaming platforms, nonprofits can now cast a wider net and appeal to a larger donor base. By utilizing the interactive features of streaming platforms, organizations can engender a sense of urgency and encourage immediate action from viewers. In addition to traditional methods, streaming media enables nonprofits to implement innovative fundraising strategies that leverage technology and social media integration, resulting in increased donations and support.

Lastly, streaming media possesses the potential to fortify social advocacy endeavors. By live-streaming rallies, demonstrations, and public hearings, nonprofits can heighten the visibility of pressing social issues and mobilize the public to take action. On-the-spot broadcasting of these events creates a sense of immediacy and urgency, compelling viewers to engage with the cause and become advocates themselves. By harnessing the power of streaming media, nonprofits can accelerate social change and leave a lasting impact.

To conclude, streaming media has revolutionized the manner in which nonprofit organizations communicate, engage, and advocate for their cause. Livestreaming events, sharing impactful stories, engaging donors and volunteers, and amplifying social advocacy efforts are just a few of the ways in which nonprofits are utilizing streaming technology. As this discussion has illustrated, streaming media has the potential to enhance the visibility, fundraising efforts, and social advocacy of nonprofit organizations. By understanding and effectively utilizing the power of streaming media, nonprofits can amplify their mission and reach a wider audience, ultimately making a greater impact in the world.

Streaming Media for Social Impact Campaigns

In recent years, streaming media has revolutionized the consumption of audio and video content, transforming the way people engage with entertainment. Platforms such as YouTube, Netflix, and Twitch have gained enormous popularity, attracting a broad audience seeking entertainment. However, it is important to recognize that streaming media also serves as a powerful tool for promoting social impact campaigns. As the Chairman and CEO of a broadcast media streaming network, I have personally witnessed the transformative power of streaming technology in driving social initiatives.

Streaming platforms offer distinct advantages for social impact campaigns, the first being their ability to reach a global audience, a challenge that traditional media outlets often struggle with. By simply sharing content with a few clicks, streaming platforms overcome geographical barriers, enabling a diverse range of individuals around the world to access and engage with social causes. This global reach is crucial for raising awareness and mobilizing support on an unprecedented scale.

Moreover, streaming platforms foster real-time interaction and engagement with audiences. Unlike traditional forms of media such as television or radio, which primarily function in a one-way manner, streaming allows for immediate feedback and dialogue between content creators and viewers. This interactivity presents social impact organizations with opportunities to engage their audience, address inquiries, and cultivate a sense of community around their cause. Through streaming media, awareness is not only raised, but a network of actively involved supporters is also built, facilitating the creation of positive change.

A prominent example of the effectiveness of streaming media in social impact campaigns is the "Hope for Education" initiative. This collaboration between a major streaming platform and educational organizations aimed to combat educational inequalities experienced by underprivileged children in rural communities. The campaign incorporated live-streamed events that shed light on the challenges faced by these children and showcased successful interventions that can make a difference.

Live-streamed events featured interviews with education experts, testimonials from students, and interactive discussions with viewers. This immersive approach allowed viewers to gain an in-depth understanding of the issues and encouraged them to take action. Additionally, the streaming platform incorporated a donation feature, providing viewers with the opportunity to contribute directly to the cause. By raising significant funds for educational programs and sparking a national dialogue on equal access to education, the campaign generated tangible impact.

Another noteworthy example is the "Justice for All" streaming campaign. Spearheaded by a coalition of social impact organizations and in partnership with a prominent streaming platform, this initiative sought to address systemic injustices faced by marginalized communities. The campaign focused on live-streaming powerful documentaries, panel discussions, and testimonials that shed light on various social issues, ranging from racial discrimination to economic disparities.

The interactive nature of the streaming platform facilitated viewer participation through live chat and social media engagement, fostering a strong sense of empowerment and solidarity among participants. This collective action and advocacy led to a broader audience and amplified the voices of marginalized communities. Through leveraging the platform's recommendation algorithms, the campaign ensured that the content reached individuals who may not have previously been exposed to these social issues. As a result, the campaign set the groundwork for meaningful change.

It should also be noted that streaming media has played a vital role in disaster relief efforts and humanitarian campaigns. When natural disasters occur or humanitarian crises unfold, streaming platforms offer real-time updates, emergency alerts, and fundraising initiatives. By broadcasting live from affected areas, people worldwide can witness the magnitude of the situation and are encouraged to contribute to relief efforts.

For instance, during a devastating earthquake in a remote location, a streaming platform collaborated with humanitarian organizations to provide live coverage of relief operations. Viewers could observe interviews with rescuers, witness the impact of their donations, and engage in conversations with volunteers on-site. This transparency and immediacy cultivated a powerful sense of empathy and solidarity, resulting in a surge of donations and support.

In conclusion, streaming media has proven to be an exceptionally effective tool for social impact campaigns. The global reach, interactive capabilities, and real-time engagement of streaming platforms make them a potent force for raising awareness, driving donations, and mobilizing communities for social causes. By harnessing the potential of streaming technology, social impact organizations can amplify their campaigns, facilitate meaningful change, and contribute to the development of a more equitable and compassionate world.

Chapter 24: Streaming Media and Virtual Communities

Streaming Media and Virtual Communities

In this chapter, an in-depth exploration will be conducted on the impact of streaming media on virtual communities, delving into the various ways it contributes to their formation and cohesion. Through rigorous research and analysis, the objective is to provide a comprehensive understanding of the role streaming media plays in shaping these virtual communities and the broader implications for society.

To begin, let us first examine the concept of virtual communities. These are social groups that primarily exist online, uniting individuals based on shared interests, values, or activities. These communities transcend geographical limitations, enabling people from all over the globe to connect. Streaming media serves as a catalyst in facilitating this connection by providing a platform for individuals to share and consume content in real-time.

One of the primary ways in which streaming media contributes to the formation of virtual communities is through the option of live streaming. This feature enables individuals to broadcast events, activities, or conversations in real-time to a widespread audience. This immersive experience fosters a sense of belonging and shared participation, cultivating a community of individuals who are connected through a common interest.

For instance, gaming communities have thrived through live streaming platforms such as Twitch. Gamers can observe their favorite players in real-time, engage with them through live chat, and even participate in multiplayer games together. This level of interactivity and real-time engagement cultivates a strong sense of camaraderie among gamers, creating a virtual community that transcends geographical boundaries.

Furthermore, streaming media empowers individuals to create and distribute user-generated content, actively contributing to the virtual communities they belong to. Platforms like YouTube allow individuals to create videos on subjects they are passionate about and share them with a global audience. Other members of the community can then engage with these videos through interaction options such as likes, comments, and shares, fostering a sense of support and connection. This participatory nature of streaming media cultivates a community that celebrates creativity and recognizes the value of individual contributions.

Streaming media not only contributes to the formation of virtual communities but also plays a crucial role in their cohesion. Through streaming media, virtual communities can engage in real-time interactions, fostering a sense of togetherness and shared experiences. This is particularly evident in the context of live events, where individuals can simultaneously watch and discuss the event, experiencing it collectively despite physical separation.

For example, consider music festivals. In the past, attending a music festival required physical presence at the venue. However, with the advent of streaming media, festivals can now be enjoyed by a global audience. People from different parts of the world can tune in to live streams of the festival, creating a shared experience and a sense of community among music enthusiasts. Through features like live chat and integration with social media platforms, viewers can interact with each other, share their excitement, and even discover new artists to explore.

Streaming media has thus transformed music festivals into virtual communities, connecting individuals who share a common love for music.

Moreover, streaming media facilitates the formation of specialized virtual communities centered around specific interests or activities. With a diverse range of streaming platforms available, individuals can find communities tailored to their unique passions, whether it be cooking, fitness, or even knitting. These niche communities provide a space for like-minded individuals to connect, share knowledge, and seek validation. The real-time nature of streaming media allows for immediate feedback, creating a dynamic and engaging environment. For instance, cooking enthusiasts can tune in to live cooking shows, interact with the host, and ask questions in real-time. This not only enhances the learning experience but also fosters a sense of belonging and camaraderie among community members who share a common passion.

In addition, streaming media contributes to the perception of authenticity and transparency within virtual communities. By offering a platform for individuals to share their lives, experiences, and perspectives, streaming media enables a deeper level of connection and understanding. These glimpses into the lives of others foster empathy and promote a sense of community built on genuine human connections.

To summarize, streaming media has indubitably revolutionized the landscape of virtual communities, fundamentally transforming the way individuals connect and interact online. Through live streaming, user-generated content, real-time interactions, and niche communities, streaming media unites people based on shared interests, fostering a sense of belonging and community. As the CEO of a broadcast media streaming network, harnessing the power of streaming media to create and strengthen virtual communities is a perpetual endeavor, enriching the lives of individuals worldwide. By comprehending the profound impact of streaming media on virtual communities, we can harness its potential to establish connections, facilitate meaningful interactions, and promote a more inclusive and interconnected society.

Chapter 25: Future of Streaming Media

AI and Personalization

As we delve further into the realm of streaming media, it becomes apparent that AI plays a vital role in augmenting user experiences. The power of AI lies in its capacity to intelligently analyze substantial volumes of data and offer personalized recommendations that cater to individual preferences. Whether it pertains to music, movies, or television shows, AI has revolutionized the manner in which we consume media.

One of the most noteworthy advancements facilitated by AI in streaming media is personalized recommendations. Gone are the days of aimlessly scrolling through endless catalogs of content, hoping to chance upon something that piques our interest. With AI algorithms at the helm, streaming platforms can now scrutinize our viewing habits, preferences, and even our mood in order to curate a collection of content specifically tailored to our inclinations.

For instance, the algorithms employed by distinguished streaming services like Netflix and Spotify devote efforts to studying our viewing or listening history, endeavoring to identify patterns and similarities among users. Subsequently, employing machine learning techniques, they extrapolate insights from these patterns to predict our potential preferences for future viewing or listening. The outcome is a personalized recommendation system that seems to comprehend our inclinations better than we comprehend them ourselves.

Content curation is another domain that shines a light on AI's capabilities. In this era of information overload, discovering content that aligns with our interests can be an overwhelming task. Nevertheless, AI-powered content curation diminishes this overwhelm by sifting through the vast sea of information and presenting us with content that is highly likely to appeal to our sensibilities.

Streaming platforms leverage AI algorithms not only to analyze our personal preferences but also to assess the preferences of multitudes of other users. This enables them to identify trends and recommend content that is currently popular or trending. By harnessing AI for content curation, streaming platforms can cater to the diverse tastes and interests of their users, thereby guaranteeing that there is something to captivate every individual.

AI's utilization in streaming media expands beyond the realm of recommendations and content curation. It extends to the analysis of user behavior and engagement. By scrutinizing user interactions with content, AI algorithms accumulate significant insights for streaming platforms and content creators. These insights can then be used to optimize user experiences and generate content that resonates deeply with audiences.

For example, AI can track the time users spend on each video, identify moments where users pause or rewind, and observe interactions within the video player interface. This data subsequently empowers streaming platforms to ascertain patterns and trends, informing their decisions on what aspects of their content are most engaging or what improvements can be made to enhance user satisfaction. It enables content creators to fashion data-driven decisions that yield superior content and improved user experiences.

AI's impact on streaming media surpasses the mere enhancement of user experiences—it has the potential to revolutionize content creation itself. Equipped with AI-powered tools and technologies, content creators can automate various processes, such as video editing or sound mixing, thereby rendering their workflows more efficient and permitting them to focus on their creative vision.

AI-powered content creation systems possess the capability to analyze copious amounts of data and generate personalized content tailored to user preferences. For instance, by analyzing a user's viewing habits, AI can generate a distinct video reel that amalgamates their favorite moments from different movies or TV shows. This personalized content creation not only enhances the user experience but also opens up new possibilities for content creators to forge deeper connections with their audience.

However, as we bear witness to the burgeoning influence of AI in the media industry, ethical considerations assume paramount significance. The employment of AI in streaming media gives rise to questions concerning user privacy, data security, algorithm biases, and the potential for AI to manipulate or shape the content we consume.

The collection and analysis of user data by AI algorithms serve as the foundation for their ability to provide personalized recommendations and content curation. While this has the potential to enhance user experiences, it also raises concerns about the privacy and security of user data. Streaming platforms must ensure the implementation of robust data protection measures and adhere to ethical guidelines when collecting and utilizing user data.

Algorithm biases represent another pertinent issue that warrants attention. AI algorithms are only as unbiased as the data on which they are trained. If the data employed to train these algorithms is inherently biased, the ensuing recommendations or content curation may perpetuate stereotypes, discrimination, or exclusion. Streaming platforms must remain vigilant in addressing and rectifying such biases and ensure that their AI systems promote diversity and inclusivity.

Furthermore, the capability of AI to manipulate or shape the content we consume raises concerns regarding the authenticity and integrity of media. As AI continues to advance, there exists the risk of AI-generated content becoming indistinguishable from content created by humans. This blurring of lines between human and AI creativity necessitates transparency and accountability within the media industry.

In conclusion, AI has substantially transformed the landscape of streaming media, revolutionizing the manner in which we discover and consume content. Whether it is through personalized recommendations, content curation, user behavior analysis, or even content creation, AI has proven to be an exceedingly formidable tool in enhancing user experiences. Nonetheless, as AI becomes further integrated into the media industry, it is imperative to address the ethical considerations surrounding its usage. By placing user privacy, data security, and algorithmic biases at the forefront, we can ensure that AI remains a consequential force for positive change within the streaming media landscape.

Immersive Media Experiences

The concept of virtual reality has been present for several decades, but recent advancements in technology have brought it closer to attaining mainstream adoption. Through the creation of simulated environments that allow for exploration and interaction, virtual reality (VR) holds great potential to revolutionize multiple industries, including gaming and education. It envisions a future where individuals can experience walking through ancient Rome, exploring the depths of the ocean, or even venturing into distant galaxies, all from the comfort of their own homes. These possibilities truly seem infinite.

Research has indicated that immersive gaming experiences can have a profound effect on players. In a study conducted by Stanford University, participants who engaged in a VR game exhibited higher levels of empathy towards the virtual character they controlled. This finding suggests that VR has the capacity to foster empathy and understanding among users, which can significantly impact social relationships and conflict resolution.

However, VR is not limited solely to gaming. It can also revolutionize the realm of storytelling. Imagine being able to step into the shoes of beloved characters and personally encounter their adventures. This interactive style of storytelling has potential to create narratives that are significantly more immersive and engaging, blurring the distinction between fiction and reality. One can picture reading a book and physically exploring the world described within its pages or watching a movie where interaction with the characters can influence the story's outcome. The future of storytelling truly appears exciting.

On the other hand, augmented reality (AR) overlays digital information onto the real world, enhancing our perception and comprehension of the environment surrounding us. Unlike VR, which submerges individuals in a completely virtual realm, AR enriches our existing reality. An example commonly known is the game Pokemon Go, in which players can observe and capture virtual creatures in real-world locations. However, AR possesses potential that extends well beyond gaming.

Consider being able to access additional information about the people, buildings, and objects present in one's vicinity. For instance, while exploring an unfamiliar city, AR could provide historical and cultural details about each landmark, transforming our understanding and appreciation of the world. Additionally, AR could revolutionize education by offering interactive and immersive lessons that bring textbook material to life. By augmenting reality with digital information, AR has the capacity to enhance our everyday experiences and provide us with novel perspectives on the world.

Mixed reality (MR), on the other hand, combines elements of both VR and AR, creating an even more immersive and interactive experience. By merging the virtual and real worlds, MR enables users to interact with virtual objects within their physical environment. This capability holds great potential for revolutionizing design, engineering, and various other industries. Envision the ability to create and manipulate virtual objects in real-time, allowing designers and engineers to visualize and test their ideas prior to materializing them.

Yet, one of the most remarkable aspects of immersive media experiences lies in the realm of virtual social interactions. Through VR, AR, and MR, individuals can connect with others in virtual worlds, irrespective of their geographical location. This has far-reaching implications for social interactions, enabling remote attendance of meetings, concerts, and events from the comfort of one's own home. Imagine the prospect of connecting with friends and family residing on the far side of the globe, as though they were sharing physical space within the same room. The potential for virtual social experiences truly inspires awe.

However, amidst these exciting prospects, it is vital to consider the potential ethical and social implications of immersive media experiences. As with any emerging technology, concerns arise pertaining to privacy, addiction, and the blurring of boundaries between virtual and real-world interactions. It is imperative that we approach these technologies with a discerning mindset and ensure that their usage remains responsible and ethical.

In conclusion, the future of immersive media experiences appears exceedingly promising. Virtual reality, augmented reality, and mixed reality hold the potential to revolutionize gaming, storytelling, education, and social interactions. They offer the ability to transport individuals to new worlds, deepen their understanding of reality, and connect them with others in ways previously unimaginable. Nevertheless, it remains crucial to approach these technologies with caution and responsibility. The possibilities are truly endless, and the future of immersive media experiences shines brightly.

Sustainability and Green Streaming

In recent years, the streaming media industry has experienced substantial growth and has emerged as a dominant force in the entertainment sector. This significant shift in consumer behavior has resulted in a considerable ecological impact, as every aspect of streaming media contributes to the industry's carbon footprint. Therefore, it is imperative to address this issue and promote sustainable practices within the industry.

One crucial aspect of green streaming is the adoption of energy-efficient technologies. The streaming media industry heavily relies on high-performance servers and data centers, which consume a substantial amount of energy. With the increasing demand for streaming services, the energy consumption of these facilities becomes an environmental concern. However, technological advancements have led to the development of more energy-efficient server infrastructure, thereby reducing the overall carbon footprint of the streaming industry. By incorporating technologies such as virtualization, data center operators can optimize the use of hardware resources, resulting in significant reductions in energy consumption and waste generation.

Another integral part of green streaming is the utilization of renewable energy sources to power data centers and server farms. As a firm advocate for sustainability, I firmly believe that transitioning to renewable energy is crucial for mitigating the carbon footprint of the streaming media industry. The advancements made in solar, wind, and hydroelectric power have made it increasingly feasible to power large-scale operations with clean energy sources. By integrating these technologies into data centers, streaming platforms can minimize their reliance on fossil fuels and contribute to a more sustainable future.

In addition to energy-efficient technologies and renewable energy sources, optimizing content delivery is vital in achieving green streaming. Content delivery networks (CDNs) are responsible for transmitting streaming data to users worldwide. However, the traditional approach to content delivery often involves redundant data transmission and inefficient routing, leading to unnecessary energy consumption. By optimizing content delivery through innovative compression algorithms, advanced routing techniques, and caching mechanisms, CDNs can enhance efficiency and reduce the environmental impact of streaming.

Furthermore, data centers and streaming platforms can adopt sustainable practices in their physical infrastructure. Constructing eco-friendly data centers characterized by innovative cooling systems, efficient power distribution, and renewable energy integration can significantly reduce the carbon footprint of the streaming industry. Additionally, implementing recycling programs for electronic waste generated by streaming platforms and data centers can help minimize the environmental impact of electronic devices.

Moreover, green streaming initiatives can extend beyond the technical aspects of the industry. As a social entrepreneur and documentary filmmaker, I firmly believe in using the power of media to promote environmental awareness and sustainable practices. Streaming platforms have an opportunity to leverage their extensive audience reach to educate and inspire viewers about sustainability, motivating them to adopt greener lifestyles. By featuring documentaries, films, and educational content addressing environmental issues and sustainable solutions, streaming platforms can actively advocate for a more sustainable future.

In conclusion, sustainability in the streaming media industry is a pressing concern that demands attention. By embracing energy-efficient technologies, employing renewable energy sources, optimizing content delivery, and implementing sustainable practices in physical infrastructure, the industry can significantly reduce its environmental impact. Green streaming initiatives, complemented by educational campaigns and corporate social responsibility, have the potential to inspire positive change and steer consumer behavior towards a more sustainable path. As the Chairman and CEO of a broadcast media streaming network, I am deeply committed to embracing and promoting these green streaming practices to build a more sustainable future for the industry and our planet as a whole.

Glossary (Streaming Acronyms)

1. Advanced Audio Coding (AAC) is a widely utilized audio compression format known for its superior sound quality and smaller file sizes compared to previous audio codecs like MP3.
2. Audio Codec 3 (AC-3), also referred to as Dolby Digital, is a commonly employed audio compression format found in DVDs, Blu-ray discs, and digital television broadcasts.
3. Adaptive Bitrate (ABR) is a streaming technique that dynamically adjusts the video quality in real-time based on the viewer's internet connection speed, ensuring a seamless and uninterrupted streaming experience.
4. Asymmetric Digital Subscriber Line (ADSL) is a type of broadband internet connection that offers faster download speeds compared to upload speeds, making it suitable for streaming multimedia content.
5. An Application Programming Interface (API) provides a set of protocols and tools designed to seamlessly integrate different software applications and services for developers.
6. Advanced Video Coding (AVC), also known as H.264 or MPEG-4 Part 10, is a widely used video compression standard renowned for its ability to deliver high-quality video with low bitrates, making it ideal for streaming.
7. Advertising Video on Demand (AVOD) is a streaming model where viewers can access content for free but are required to watch advertisements during the streaming experience.
8. A Content Delivery Network (CDN) is a network of geographically distributed servers that store and deliver streaming content to users based on their location, ensuring faster and more reliable streaming experiences.
9. Digital Rights Management (DRM) technologies are utilized to protect copyrighted content from unauthorized access, distribution, and piracy.
10. Digital Terrestrial Television (DTT) is a broadcasting technology that utilizes a digital format to deliver television signals over the airwaves instead of analog.
11. Digital Video Broadcasting (DVB) is a suite of international standards used for digital television transmission, encompassing satellite, cable, and terrestrial broadcasting.

12. Digital Video Recorders (DVRs) enable users to record and store television programs for later playback, providing them with control over their viewing schedules.

13. An Electronic Program Guide (EPG) is an on-screen menu that offers viewers information about current and upcoming television programs, facilitating navigation and scheduling of viewing.

14. Full High Definition (FHD) pertains to a display resolution of 1920 x 1080 pixels, providing sharp and detailed picture quality for streaming video content.

15. Frames Per Second (FPS) measures the number of individual frames displayed per second in a video, with higher FPS resulting in smoother and more lifelike motion.

16. File Transfer Protocol (FTP) is a standard network protocol used for transferring files from one computer to another over a TCP/IP-based network.

17. High Definition (HD) refers to a display resolution higher than standard definition, offering clearer and more detailed picture quality.

18. HTTP Live Streaming (HLS) is a streaming protocol developed by Apple that uses adaptive bitrate streaming to deliver live and on-demand video content over the internet.

19. Hypertext Markup Language Version 5 (HTML5) is the most recent version of the standard markup language utilized for creating web pages and applications, providing advanced multimedia capabilities, including video streaming.

20. Hypertext Transfer Protocol (HTTP) is an application protocol used for transmitting hypertext over the internet, serving as the foundation for accessing and delivering web-based content, including streaming media.

21. The Interactive Advertising Bureau (IAB) is an industry association responsible for setting standards and providing guidance for the digital advertising industry, including streaming platforms.

22. Internet Protocol Television (IPTV) is a system that delivers TV programs and video content over the internet, enabling viewers to stream content on-demand or in real-time.

23. Integrated Services Digital Network (ISDN) is a telecommunications network infrastructure that offers digital voice, video, and data services over traditional copper phone lines.

24. Joint Photographic Experts Group (JPEG) is a widely used image compression format that allows for high-quality images with relatively small file sizes, making it suitable for streaming.

25. A Local Area Network (LAN) is a network that connects computers and devices within a limited area, such as a home, office, or school, facilitating resource and information sharing.

26. A Learning Management System (LMS) is a software application used to create, manage, and deliver e-learning courses, including streaming video lectures and tutorials.

27. Megabits Per Second (Mbps) is a unit of measurement indicating the speed at which data can be transferred, conveying the amount of data that can be transmitted in one second.

28. Multi-Bitrate (MBR) is a streaming technique that encodes a single video file into multiple bitrates, allowing the player to switch between different bitrates based on the viewer's internet connection speed.

29. The Moving Picture Experts Group (MPEG) is a standards body responsible for developing audio and video compression formats, including MPEG-2, MPEG-4, and MPEG-7, which are widely used in streaming.

30. A Multiple System Operator (MSO) is a company that owns and operates multiple cable or satellite television systems, bundling services like internet, television, and phone.

31. Over-The-Top (OTT) refers to the delivery of audio, video, and other media content over the internet, bypassing traditional broadcast networks.

32. Peer-To-Peer (P2P) is a decentralized network architecture where computers and devices connect directly to each other, enabling the sharing of files and streaming content without reliance on a centralized server.

33. A Personal Computer (PC) is a general-purpose computer designed for individual use, including streaming multimedia content.

34. Pixels Per Inch (PPI) measures the density of pixels in a display, indicating the sharpness and clarity of images and videos.

35. Quadrature Amplitude Modulation (QAM) is a modulation scheme employed in cable television systems to transmit digital signals over coaxial cables.

36. Quality of Service (QoS) refers to the measurement and management of network performance, ensuring smooth and reliable delivery of streaming content.

37. A Request for Proposal (RFP) is a document used to solicit proposals from potential vendors or service providers, including streaming technology solutions.

38. Real-Time Messaging Protocol (RTMP) is a streaming protocol developed by Adobe for the real-time delivery of audio, video, and data over the internet.

39. Standard Definition (SD) refers to a display resolution lower than high definition, offering lower-quality picture compared to HD or FHD.

40. Secure Reliable Transport (SRT) is an open-source streaming protocol that combines the benefits of UDP-based transport with the reliability of TCP, ensuring secure and low-latency video delivery.

41. Server-Side Ad Insertion (SSAI) is a technique used to seamlessly insert targeted advertisements into streaming content on the server-side, enabling smooth transitions and personalization.

42. A Set-Top Box (STB) is a device that receives and decodes television signals, allowing users to access and control streaming content on their televisions.

43. Scalable Video Coding (SVC) is a video compression standard that enables the delivery of video at multiple resolutions and bitrates, facilitating adaptive streaming.

44. Subscription Video on Demand (SVOD) is a streaming model where viewers pay a recurring subscription fee to access a library of content without any advertisements.

45. Transmission Control Protocol (TCP) is a reliable and connection-oriented protocol used for the transmission of data over IP-based networks, ensuring error-free delivery of streaming content.

46. User Datagram Protocol (UDP) is an unreliable and connectionless protocol used for the transmission of data over IP-based networks, suitable for real-time streaming applications.

47. Ultra High Definition (UHD) refers to a display resolution higher than high definition, offering a more detailed and immersive visual experience.

48. A Uniform Resource Locator (URL) is the web address specifying the location of a resource, like a webpage or a streaming video file, on the internet.

49. User Experience (UX) refers to the overall experience and satisfaction that users have when interacting with a website, application, or streaming service.

50. Variable Bitrate (VBR) is a streaming technique that adjusts the bitrate of the video based on the complexity of the content, resulting in improved video quality and smaller file sizes.

51. Video on Demand (VOD) refers to a streaming model where viewers can access and watch video content at their convenience, commonly through subscription-based platforms.

52. A Virtual Private Network (VPN) is a secure and private network connection that enables users to access the internet and stream content anonymously and securely.

53. Virtual Reality (VR) is a simulated experience that can resemble or differ from the real world, offering viewers immersive and interactive streaming experiences.

54. Variable Refresh Rate (VRR) is a display technology that synchronizes the monitor's refresh rate with the output of the streaming device, reducing screen tearing and enhancing image quality.

55. A Web Application Firewall (WAF) is a security tool that analyzes and filters web traffic to protect streaming platforms and applications from cyber threats and attacks.

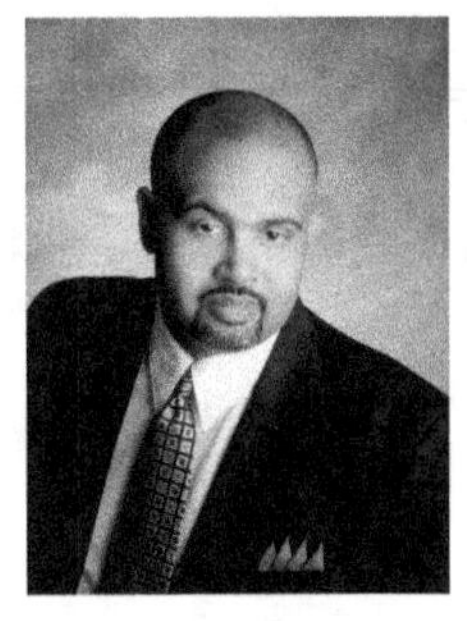

Dr. Myron A. Raney is an Interdisciplinary Researcher, Documentary Film Maker, and Emeritus College Professor. He is the Chairman and C.E.O. of Bufe Tv, Incorporated, which is a Global Broadcast Streaming Network headquartered in Columbus, Ohio. To his credit, Dr. Raney is the host of the One Nation Under Deviance radio show that premiers primetime Saturday mornings on 1580 The Praise radio. His current research interest includes research in the Social and Behavioral Sciences that examines societies social problems and relevant deviant behaviors utilizing Government Failure Theory as the theoretical lens to identify the root causes, discover opportunities for nonprofit organizations, and develop faith-based programs for impactful social service delivery.

He is considered to be an expert in both qualitative and quantitative analysis using documentary, ethnographic, and videographic research models as well as meta-analysis and meta-synthesis. It is his experience as a researcher, educator, and corporate executive that gives him the knowledge and insight to lend credible knowledge to this book.

In his spare time Dr. Raney enjoys traveling internationally and attending professional sporting events with his family and friends. He is married to his beautiful wife Marites, and they have six children: Shirlean, Charmaine, Makayla, Maulo, Carlo, and Mycah. They also have four grandchildren: Zane, Dane, Wayne, and Amory; as well as two grand-puppies, Nazier and Cash.